ALEXANDER ALLAND, JR., is Professor of Anthropology at Columbia University. He is a graduate of the University of Wisconsin and received his Ph.D. in anthropology from Yale University. Professor Alland has done extensive field work in both Africa and the United States. He was awarded a John Simon Guggenheim fellowship for 1976–77 to enable him to study children's art in the Far East. Professor Alland has taught at Vassar College, the University of Connecticut, and Hunter College. He is married and has two children.

The Artistic Animal

AN INQUIRY INTO
THE BIOLOGICAL ROOTS
OF ART

Alexander Alland, Jr.

1977
Anchor Books
Anchor Press/Doubleday
Garden City, New York

Grateful acknowledgment is made for permission to include excerpts from the following copyrighted publications:

A *Nice and Abstruse Game* by Harold Schonberg. Copyright © 1962 by American Heritage Publishing Company, Inc. Reprinted by permission of Horizon Publications, January, 1962.

Louis-Ferdinand Céline, *Death on the Installment Plan*, translated by Ralph Manheim. Copyright Librarie Gallimard 1952, © 1966 by Ralph Manheim. Reprinted by permission of New Directions Publishing Corporation.

From *Ingalik Social Culture* by C. Osgood. Reprinted by courtesy of Yale University Publications in Anthropology, Vol. 53.

From *Profile of Robert Rauschenberg* by Calvin Tomkins. First appeared in *The New Yorker*, February 29, 1964, issue. Reprinted by permission of New Yorker Magazine, Inc.

From "The Relationship of the Poet to Day-Dreaming", in *Collected Papers, Sigmund Freud*, Vol. 4, edited by Ernest Jones, M.D., authorized translation under the supervision of Joan Riviere. Published by Basic Books, Inc., by arrangement with The Hogarth Press, Ltd., and the Institute of Psycho-Analysis, London.

Library of Congress Cataloging in Publication Data

Alland, Alexander, 1931–
The artistic animal.

Bibliography
Includes index.
1. Creation (Literary, artistic, etc.)
2. Arts—Psychology. I. Title.
NX165.A455   700'.1
Library of Congress Catalog Card Number: 76-53408
ISBN: 0-385-09771-9

For Ruth Bunzel

Colleague, Friend, and Pioneer
in the Anthropology of Art

Contents

Preface

Every human being is the result of a unique combination of genes and the interaction between these genes and a personal history. These act together to produce the whole person. Yet genetic potentialities, built into our brains, can generate artistic behavior in the sense of both creation and appreciation. This exclusively human pattern determines an infinite space within which individual creativity can achieve its full expression. It is this space that I explore in *The Artistic Animal*.

I have not used a specific definition of art in this book. When I refer to art I mean all of the fine arts, including visual art, music, literature, dance, theatre, film, and the mixed media. Neither have I used the word "beauty" except in Chapter 2, in order to contrast "beautiful" with "ugly" subject matter, and in Chapter 7 to distinguish between what is judged as a beautiful painting and what is judged as a beautiful sunset. In the latter case I recognize that beauty can, but need not be, one criterion that figures in artistic appreciation. "Aesthetic" is used only in the following sense: appreciative of, or responsive to, form in art or nature. This definition is borrowed in revised form from the third usage of aesthetic found in Webster's New Collegiate Dictionary, which reads: "appreciative of, or responsive to, the beautiful in art or nature. . . ." I have shifted ground away from "beauty" to the "appreciation of form." The latter term is used throughout to delimit "pattern or schema" and "good form" is used in reference to those forms that produce the aesthetic response in "sensitive" individuals. *Aesthetic response* is, therefore, a response to form and is taken to be one of the basic emotions in the human species.

Although this book is my own, its origin and existence are based on a long series of debts. I wish to thank my wife, Sonia, for many helpful suggestions and for encouraging me to rewrite sections that she correctly saw as unclear or illogical. The same applies to my editor at Doubleday/Anchor, Elizabeth Knappman, who has guided this book through its many revisions. I also owe a great debt to my students, but particularly to Larry Hirschfield, Rena Lederman, and John Hennessey. They all read my first draft with great care and made many useful criticisms.

All illustrations, except the chimpanzee painting, are by the author from his own collection. Professor Herbert Terrace graciously provided the chimpanzee painting.

Alexander Alland, Jr.

The Artistic Animal

Chapter 1

The Artistic Space

SEVERAL YEARS AGO, in New York City, the painter Robert Rauschenberg asked his friend Willem de Kooning to give him a drawing. "What do you want it for?" asked De Kooning. "I want to erase it," responded Rauschenberg. According to Calvin Tomkins, whose long "Profile" of Rauschenberg in *The New Yorker* (February 29, 1964) is my source for this story, De Kooning's first impulse was to refuse the request. He saw it as destruction, while Rauschenberg saw the process as a means for the creation of a new work. Rauschenberg argued his case convincingly and De Kooning finally gave in. "He pulled out one drawing, looked at it, and said, 'No, I'm not going to make it easy for you. It has to be something I'd miss.' Then he took out another portfolio, and looked through that and finally gave me a drawing, and I took it home. It wasn't easy, by any means. The drawing was done with hard line, and it was greasy, too, so I had to work very hard on it, using every sort of eraser. But in the end it really worked. I *liked* the result. I felt it was a legitimate work of art created by the technique of erasing."

The finished work entitled *Erased de Kooning* and signed Robert Rauschenberg has been shown in several public exhibitions.

Several years ago, also in New York City, a teen-ager armed with a felt-tipped pen began to write his nickname and house number on the walls and subway cars of the city. The idea soon became a fad. By the early seventies "subway graffiti" had exploded into an art form. Spray paint, which quickly replaced the felt-tipped pen as the favorite medium, provided a quick means of attacking a large surface. Colorful signatures spread over the walls, doors, and sometimes the windows of the city's subway cars. The nicknames (cryptic to the police and the general public, but known to many of the artists and their friends) provided the common basis of design which was elaborated by each artist according to individual style. City authorities, particularly the mayor, were outraged by what they considered acts of public vandalism. Millions of dollars were spent each year to remove the graffiti.

Both the illegality of the act and the cleaning process undoubtedly stimulate the production of more spectacular and more numerous paintings. Each artist has to work fast in order to avoid arrest. The greater the surface covered and the greater the number of paintings completed, the longer the work of an individual will persist. This is action painting born of necessity. Cleaned cars provide renewed surfaces for more graffiti.

The cleaning process has contributed in another and more direct way to subway art. Many of the colors used are quite fast. Only complete repainting will totally obliterate well-applied graffiti. As a result muted, ghostlike shapes and colors of erased graffiti continue to speed down New York's subway tunnels. I have no doubt that these erasures, an instance of life imitating art, please many New Yorkers other than myself—Rauschenberg and De Kooning among them.

The nineteenth-century Impressionist revolution and the initial response of public and critics to it are well known. Since the middle of the century the art public has been blitzed by a series of "revolutions" in style and direction, which have, each in their time, become the safe background for what many considered more and more outrageous assaults upon the canons of art. With the invention of photography, many painters and sculptors turned their backs on realism to explore overtly what had covertly been the concern of artists at least since the Renaissance. Light, form, and color, as well as the relation of these to emotional expression, became, in varying degrees and varying ways, the subject matter of art. Along with post-Impressionism and Expressionism, a new "realism" developed which probed the unconscious and presented either photographic or expressionistic representations of our inner symbolic life. Surrealism led naturally to a break with traditional media, and all kinds of found objects came to be incorporated into artistic production. The New York School in the 1950s defined art as process. A finished painting was the kinetic residue of action. The act of painting, frozen on the canvas, became the focus of artistic presence.

As the number of modern artists and their productivity grew, scarcity and value were maintained by an increasing demand for competent innovation and originality. The affluent fifties and sixties saw a series of schools pass rapidly through the galleries. Free abstraction which had reached its peak of energy with the action school yielded to the camp realism of "pop art" and the controlled geometry of "op art." The notion of "action" reached its logical climax in "happenings" as experimental ideas led to the simultaneous erosion of the boundaries between artist and spectator and between one medium and another. In the midst of all this innovation, the challenge thrown down by Marcel Duchamp just before he died in 1968 that the museum of the future would be an empty loft was taken up by the "minimal school," which used simple everyday objects and, without transforming them, physically converted them to art through contextual placement in gallery or museum.

Pop art was a conscious recognition of the impact of mass culture on our senses. It transformed the objects and images of everyday life through a series of processes ranging from enlarged hamburgers (Claes Oldenburg's *Floorburger*, for example) to soft telephones or the hauntingly real-unreal life casts by George Segal. In the latter, white plaster figures are positioned among real but cast-off props taken from such everyday material as run-down coffee shops or discarded buses.

Pop art and minimal art are both the arts of the mundane—the mundane transformed either through the manipulation of one or more aspects of the real object or image, or through placement in a context which defines art almost by an act of defiance.

The direct descendant of these two schools (but also opposed to them) is "hyperrealism," in which the human figure is "exactly" reproduced. Hyperrealist sculpture is so real that it has led to a revolution in the technical reproduction of figures for those marginal art forms found in wax museums, the focus of which has been "living" history.

The final transmogrification of the silent wax works of Madame Tussaud (popular hyperrealism) comes appropriately enough in the technological wizardry of Disneyland in California and Walt Disney's World in Florida. There, things move!

4

The illusion is complete! The Cretaceous period is re-created in detail. Spectators seated in robot trams, Disney's substitute for time machines, watch plastic death battles between Tyrannosaurus and Triceratops or float down a man-made segment of an African river in a power boat which swerves at the last moment to avoid a vinyl hippo rising on cue to scare those who have paid to be taken in by it all. Now and then a real bird invades this substitute world. The spectator is caught off guard. Is it real? Yes, but its presence in the make believe context reduces it to the status of a prop against which the hyperreality of plastic animals is confirmed. In one sense, life becomes art.

The Disney worlds create several realities. Visitors may explore the distant past when dinosaurs roamed the earth, cross through the technological marvels of the present, and enter the future by way of a three-dimensional realization of science fiction. Which hyperreality one chooses is a matter of taste, but all offer a momentary escape into a universe populated by living toys.

The bunraku puppet theater of Japan is another kind of hyperreality involving drama and music. The bunraku puppets are about three-quarters life size and so realistic that they appear to move with all the grace of well-trained dancers. So complex are the mechanisms in these puppets that it takes three skilled operators to animate each one of them. Dressed in black with black hoods and gloves they cluster around each character in the play but are ignored by the audience. The reality of the puppets contrasts with the artificial means by which they are manipulated. Even more striking is the conscious stylization of the performance. Everything is calculated to provide distance. Musicians and actors sit to one side of the stage, well away from the dramatic action. The puppets perform against sche-

5

matic backdrops. Parts are sung in a stylized manner as each performer reads from a clearly visible text.

For a Western observer the performance breaks into two equally intense centers of focus. The bunraku theater has undoubtedly been constructed to contrast a single, controlled, artificial reality (the puppets) on the one hand, with artificial stylization on the other. The puppets, after all, are artificial and the humans real. Yet the puppets move as if they were living people and the performers act mechanically. A series of transformations thus vibrate back and forth between human performance and animation.

Although the plays deal with believable human experience, as theater, bunraku draws its audience into the performance by creating a suspension of reality. This same process occurs in much of Western theater, but the bunraku uses a set of artifices which gives it a special character.

The French newspaper *Le Monde* for June 12, 1974, described the bunraku theater as follows:

> Depersonalized animators become the mechanisms that breathe a simulated and disincarnated life into these perfect reproductions of human beings.
>
> It is a strange sorcery, a super-Brechtian dream of distance and dissociation. All the elements of the spectacle are given simultaneously but are separated spatially. The eye sees them apart, but the observer is forced to reunify them. When a character in a play reaches for a scroll, a hand gloved in black is superimposed over the delicate articulations of the minute fingers. Whose fingers are they? The manipulator and the puppet are confused in the same action. When a battle scene unfolds, it becomes a melee of black phantoms and puppets from which, it appears, come the cries and roars. (Translation mine.)

The Artistic Space

Puppets are a popular theater form in much of the world. They are common in Europe and shadow puppets are found in a wide arc from Egypt and Turkey in the Middle East, through India, China, Japan, Thailand, Vietnam, Java, and Bali in the Far East. Three-dimensional doll puppets are also found in several of these regions.

That theater people in these cultures are aware of the transformational aspect inherent in puppets is illustrated by an old saying among Burmese dancers quoted in *Intermezzo*, the magazine of Carnegie Hall for September/October 1975: ". . . when a human dancer dances he must be like a puppet, and when the puppet dances he must be like a human dancer."

Theater, ritual, and dance employing masks have an even wider distribution than puppetry. They are found throughout Europe and Asia, as well as in Africa and much of the New World. In a ritual context, the use of puppets and masks serves to produce a conscious religious transformation: mortal (as performer) into god or spirit. This transformation is frequently aided by a long period of ceremonial prayer and meditation that precedes a performance and which takes place off stage and in private. This "taking on," or personification, of supernatural personae can be seen in another form in the possessionlike trance states that are found in many ceremonies, particularly in Africa and South Asia.

In all of these cases, the ritual effect is clearly enhanced by the material and spiritual transformation of its participants, for the transformation is a means of making religious beliefs immediate and concrete. Transformation, however, is also a major feature of all secular theater. Think how boring and undramatic a slice of real life would be on stage. Even *cinéma vérité* which pretends to present life "as it is" is heavily controlled in the cutting room. If *cinéma vérité* is art, it is so precisely because it is life manipulated and transformed by its director-editor.

In Jean-Luc Godard's film *La Chinoise* a male character takes the seat and handlebars from a bicycle and uses them as the head and horns of a bull. A mock bullfight takes place between the man and a female character. Soon they tire of the game and the "bull's head" is discarded just outside the door of the apartment in which the action takes place. Before they shut the door a man comes up the stairs, spies the discarded bicycle parts, and says, "Oh. A perfectly good bike seat and handlebars." He takes them and walks away. The woman turns to her companion. "What did the man say?" she asks. Her companion replies, "He's a genius. He can make a bike seat and handlebars from a bull's head."

La Chinoise is in many ways a film about language and art. The scene just described involves the transformation of a mundane object into something else, a bull's head. The bicycle parts function in the fantasy situation like found objects in an art gallery.

Transformation of the mundane is a prime requisite of drama. Transformation is also the major artifice on which all art is built. As the Austro-British art historian Ernst Gombrich has pointed out, art, even the most realistic art, is illusion. Realism is, in fact, a goal that is limited to certain periods of Western art, and even then it is unattainable. A look at the art of preliterate cultures shows how little other traditions are concerned with producing a copy of a person or object.

The artist is the master of sleight of hand. The Swedish director Ingmar Bergman's film *The Magician* explores this precise point, as well as the connection between art and ritual or ceremony. In non-Western cultures religious belief helps the audience to accept artistic and ritual transformations. The artist is either a participant in ritual or plays a major role in the preparation of ritual paraphernalia. In modern Western art new techniques are constantly sought in order to render the illusion, as well as the form, fresh and immediate. If the art is to work, the artist's sleight of hand must catch its audience off guard. Even chance events can be mobilized to serve the artist in this way.

The American Merce Cunningham dances to a reading from the autobiographical notes of the composer John Cage. Each time the dance is performed, the selections are chosen at random. Different passages are used in different performances. Oddly enough, the text never goes against the dance; often it appears to have been chosen specifically for a set of movements in the piece. This type of happy accident pleases both Cunningham and Cage, who frequently allow chance to play a role in their compositions. One night during a performance in Paris of a dance called *Landrover* a woman in the audience got up and, as she left the hall, said in English, "This is the worst shit I have ever seen." A few minutes later her words, which had been picked up on Cage's tape recorder, appeared as part of the score. In another of Cunningham's dances, *Winterbranch*, the stage is lit only intermittently and even then, poorly. The audience is forced to peer intently into the dark. Some give up; others find the experience highly intense. The latter are compelled to participate by their effort to see what is happening on stage. They are pulled into the performance just as believers are pulled into a ritual.

Transformation in visual art must take place in the spatial arrangement or color of a work. In the theater or films, and in literature to some extent, the artist is also free to manipulate time. In most theater, time is compressed, but the temporal element can be distorted in other ways.

Bob Wilson, a new young American playwright, slows down the action in his theater pieces. The shortest last all night, the longest have run nonstop for over a week. Characters in these plays often appear to move through thick glue. The transformation of time gives them an immediate surrealistic dimension. Wilson is one of the few people working in live theater who can create the kind of dream world so possible in film. His plays are constructed out of several unrelated scenes. Parts of one play may appear unchanged in another. *The Life and Times of Joseph Stalin* runs for twelve hours. Among the many acts are one which takes place on a beach, another in a Victorian drawing room, and another in a cave full of animals. Continuity is provided by a runner in a track suit who passes across the back of the stage from time to time as the play unfolds.

Wilson is rightly seen as an innovator in modern theater, but his treatment of time is a familiar element of most non-Western ritual. While our own religious ceremonies usually take place in the course of a single morning or evening, so called "primitives" often spin them out to enormous lengths.

The Ingalik Indians, northern Athabaskans who live in Western Canada, have a ritual performance, the animal ceremony, which lasts for seventeen nights. The purpose of the animal ceremony is to increase the food supply. It involves a series of dances, songs, and skits performed primarily by a song leader and four major characters identified by their characteristic masks. The red male and red female masks are the most important. The Ingalik name given to the red masks means "to go at night." This denotes the fact that most red mask dances take place after supper. To act as a red mask character of either sex is a privilege which is inherited through the male line.

Second in importance to the red masks are the black masks.

These are both male, but one is the older and the other the younger brother. The Ingalik name for these masks is "to go in the daytime." The black masks take part in the ceremony mostly in the afternoon and they are the clowns of the piece.

There are two other unpaired masks, which are of funny faces and appear only on the fourteenth night of the ceremony. In addition to these stock characters, there is a large set of variable masks representing minor comic roles.

The animal ceremony consists of an ordered set of songs, dances, and skits, many of which involve the audience. The black masks remain mute; their lines are provided by members of the audience who also shout directions during much of the action. Cornelius Osgood, the Yale ethnographer, describes one of the comedy sequences as follows:

> At an appropriate time, the big black mask enters the kashim [communal house] through the door and dances around, gesturing as though he were wishing to embrace someone.
>
> "Oh, you are going to take a woman. You are getting old enough now," yells an onlooker.
>
> The big black mask hides under the bench [along the wall of the kashim].
>
> The onlookers tell the big black mask that the women have gone to bed. The latter comes out from under the bench and makes slow steps toward the corner where the women are lying, stopping and listening on the way just as a young man does who surreptitiously calls upon a girl in the night. The onlookers tell him that the women are sleeping. He goes to the bed and touches the young girl lightly.
>
> "That's the one," he is encouraged by someone in the audience.
>
> He steps back and listens. Then he returns and making a

mistake, lies down beside the old woman. He puts an arm and leg over her.

"Keep still a little while. Think what you are going to do. Don't be too rough," the audience advises.

Pretty soon he pushes the old woman and she begins to cough as an old woman coughs. The big black mask runs pretending that he is escaping from the women's house.

"You've made a mistake," say the onlookers.

The old woman shakes herself, "Who wakes me up? What's the matter with those boys? They won't leave the girls alone!" She pretends it is morning and gets up to make the breakfast fire.

A later scene unfolds as follows:

"You get fooled all the time. Don't make any mistakes tonight," he [the black mask] is advised.

The big black mask moves toward the women slowly.

"You certainly take a long time," comments an onlooker as the black mask touches the girl under the blanket in his efforts at identification. He continues cautiously because, having made so many mistakes, he is uncertain.

"Smell her breath. Put your nose in her mouth," says someone with the common assumption that an old woman's breath smells differently from a young one's.

The black mask goes to the young woman first.

"That's the old woman. Smell the other one!"

The black mask then moves around to the side of the old woman.

"Take that one. That's right."

He stands thinking how to lie down with her.

"Feel her behind. Take her pants down and sleep with her. She won't wake up any more!" The onlookers are excited and continue to offer obvious suggestions.

The big black mask pushes up the sleeves of his parka and

continues feeling the old woman. Then he pulls her trousers down and loosens his own.

The old woman wakes up and discovers that her trousers have been pulled down, whereupon she yells and attempts to catch her attacker. The big black mask breaks away but does not know which way to go, bumping into the wall while the old woman pretends to light the lamp. Finally her assailant escapes under the bench.

"What's the matter with that fellow? He bothers me every night," the old woman says to her granddaughter. "Did you tell him to come here?" The girl simply hangs her head and says nothing. They proceed with the building of the fire as usual.

The opening of the last act occurs when the two females prepare to go to bed. . . . The old woman says, "If that fellow comes in again, I am going to get sticks and hit him." At this suggestion, people in the audience throw her a number of sticks. Then the women go to bed.

The big black mask comes out once again feeling his head which had been bumped in the struggles of the night before. He listens to hear if anyone is awake.

"Try again. This time you are going to get her. Success always results on the fourth night." He goes up and touches the women. "Smell their blankets too." He smells the blankets.

In this manner he locates the young girl and as he prepares to sleep with her, the onlookers tell him, "Hold her tight even if she screams and bites you." Then he lies down beside her.

The grandmother wakes up and goes to urinate in her urine basket, scratching it to imitate the sound. Afterward she puts the basket beside her and lies down again.

"Now get up slowly," someone suggests, "and listen if the old woman is sleeping."

The black mask raises his head and listens. Then he lies

down again and grabs the girl, who screams. The old woman wakes up and tries to pull him off the girl but cannot. She hits him with sticks, but he hangs on for a while. Finally he lets go. The girl jumps over to the other side of the grandmother. The big black mask's trousers, which are loose, fall down in fighting with the old woman whose trousers are also dragging. While the conflict rages the young girl runs out, actually leaving the kashim. The old woman hits the big black mask until he is laid out on the floor. Then she picks up her urine basket and also leaves the kashim.

"You didn't get the girl and nothing but a licking. Put on medicine for yourself."

The big black mask makes the motions and jumps up well. Then he dances around the kashim as he did when he first entered and finally goes out.

The fourteenth night is the great night of the animal ceremony. People show up dressed in their best clothes. The evening begins with the ceremonial eating of "ice cream," and several mythic scenes are performed. One of these has a tragic content and is enacted by the red masks:

Having received their instructions from the song leader, the red male enters carrying a real bow and arrow while his partner brings a stuffed parka, a single arrow, and a piece of skin covered with red paint. As the singing proceeds, the red male mask comes out and goes to a position in front of the door facing the fireplace from which suddenly rises the red female mask. Close inspection, however, would show that the figure is only a straw dummy, clothed in the parka and red mask of the original. The red female mask dummy rocks four times toward each corner [of the kashim] in turn. As it does so, the red male mask pretends to shoot at it with his weapon. On the fourth bow of the dummy . . . the red male actually does so and the simulated red female, struck with the arrow, falls into the fire hole. The dummy is no sooner down, however, than the real red female rises wearing the red mask and holding an arrow to the nude upper part of the body on which red paint has been smeared and which is quite indistinguishable from blood in the dim light of the kashim.

This dance of the "murder of the woman" has dramatic meaning to the audience for the legend on which it is based has been told during periods of leisure in the previous days of the ceremony. The audience consequently knows that at a time when the red mask and his wife, whom the performers represent, were younger they had trouble because of another woman who had grown fond of the red male. The red female was resentful and quarreled with the intruder. The red male liked the other woman a little, however, and became angry at his wife for making the situation obvious. He went off hunting and on his return at nightfall the woman who liked him was waiting along the trail. Still irritated over the developments which had occurred, he thought the woman following him surreptitiously was his wife and becoming infuriated he shot her with his bow and arrow. Not until he entered his home did he realize what he had done.

The animal ceremony is a highly developed and controlled form of ritual drama. The religious function is expressed through song, dance, mime, and patterned interactions between actors and participants. Although the animal ceremony is significant as a major religious event that dramatizes the relationship between the Ingalik and nature as well as the well-being of both, it is also an event that is meant to be enjoyed. The entire sequence has the flavor of controlled spontaneity. The myths and ritual ideas that constitute this rite are transformed by means of dramatic enactment into an immediate reality. The animal ceremony helps to maintain social and religious harmony, and the amusement generated by its comic scenes are integrated into its over-all function.

The animal ceremony is a complex form of theater that shares obvious dramatic and comic effects with the secular theater of other times and places. In many respects, it resembles the *commedia dell'arte* with its comic sequences involving the use of masks, mistaken identity, and mime. Audience participation, a major feature of all ritual, is integrated directly into the event without difficulty because each Ingalik knows his or her appropriate role.

Ritual and theater both seek to establish links between performer and spectator. In our own culture, real audience participation is difficult to achieve because no direct means of involving spectators in role playing exists. Many modern innovators in the theater have attempted to re-establish a rituallike connection between audience and performers. Different artifices must be used. Merce Cunningham has employed poor lighting or his tape recorder. Bob Wilson has distorted time in an attempt to pull his audience along with the slow motion of his stage action and the rituallike length of his plays.

Theater in modern Western society is, like most of our art, cut away from a direct integration into the sacred and secular aspects of symbolic life. The theater may be about life, but it is separated from it by its function as art. In non-Western societies this is usually not the case. Art not only functions as a part of ritual, but may be understood only as a segment of a wider social whole.

The Baruya, who live in the New Guinea highlands, also have a major ceremonial cycle. Theirs involves the initiation of boys into adulthood. These ceremonies are an intervillage event and tend, along with their religious function, to unite separate settlements that have no political means for the establishment of solidarity.

Baruya initiation is long and complex. The entire sequence lasts six weeks. Although women participate in preparatory activities, Baruya women, unlike the Ingalik, have no part to play in the actual event. In fact, Baruya initiation rites dramatize the separation between mothers and their preadolescent sons which occurs at the beginning of the cycle. Young men will have no contact with their mothers again until they reach full adulthood in their twenties. Baruya society is characterized not only by this long separation, but also by manifest hostility between the sexes.

At each initiation boys of different ages move up one step in a graded series of stages. Promotion is marked by special aspects of the ceremony itself and by the adoption of special insignia, including forms of dress and nose ornaments. Elaborate grass skirts are a sign of full adulthood for males. These are made by male relatives with special materials and traditionally fixed techniques. Initiates are dressed by men.

In contrast to the initiation, which is an official and sacred ceremony, the Baruya have an event in which women, girls, and uninitiated boys participate. This is the construction of a utilitarian object, a scarecrow, which is used in the gardens around the village. While scarecrow making is in no real sense a ceremony, it stands in obvious opposition to initiation rites. Not only do the sexes participate together, but women are allowed to dress the male figure, something which is otherwise taboo within the culture. In addition, although the finished scarecrow appears to be clothed in traditional fashion, the materials used to form the costume are all studiously different from the ones used in real dress. Furthermore, the event is characterized by lightheartedness and joy. Scarecrow construction and initiation ceremonies contrast as follows:

Initiation	Scarecrow Construction
males only	women, girls, boys
sacred	secular
inter village	intra village
rite of transition	no transition
dressing of boys	dressing of scarecrow
hostility between sexes	joking between sexes
men dress boys	women and girls dress male figure
materials used correct	materials used incorrect
sacred behavior reinforcing rules	secular behavior breaking rules
serious	jovial

Scarecrow making in this case, at least, is part of a symbolic structure manifested in ritual. Like art, it involves the manipulation of symbols in a context other than ordinary, everyday language.

The examples in this chapter involve the *representation* of something by something else. All involve *transformations* of one sort or another. A drawing is already the transformation of ideas and/or reality on a two-dimensional surface. The erasure of a drawing is a further transformation and also a new representation. Certainly a De Kooning painting or drawing is something other than an erased De Kooning by Rauschenberg. Graffiti are an intentional form; their erasure produces an unintentional form. In the first case, the art is defined by the artist; in the latter, by the perceiver. Both can be art because art is in fact a social phenomenon ultimately involving artist and audience. Some modern artists, Cunningham among them, intentionally allow random elements to enter into their works. Other works become enhanced by unintentional chance events. The patina on three-thousand-year-old Shang bronzes or other forms of ancient art is an example of a more conventionally accepted unintentional enhancement, but patination is really no different from the erasure of graffiti. Erasure involves intentional obliteration but it also produces a transformation of form.

Baruya initiation transforms the content of everyday culture, producing a condensation and heightened awareness of maleness and femaleness. This is manifested by acting out set patterns of behavior through dancing, singing, and the adoption of certain dress forms which will mark the status of initiates in their daily lives as long as they remain in the grade achieved at the ceremony. The sacred sets the stage for a new status in the context of secular life. The making of a scarecrow involves the construction of an artificial form in the context of a social activity. It is a mild parody of Baruya beliefs and social structure and a further transformation of social concerns from ritual and the sacred, back to the secular scene.

The Ingalik animal ceremony is strikingly like the *commedia dell'arte* in form and like the Bob Wilson theater in duration. Duration, of course, is also an aspect of form in which temporal elements are used instead of material elements.

If the Ingalik ceremony is like the *commedia dell'arte*, the reverse is also true. What emerges from this and other comparisons is the fact that different transformational elements appear over and over in different cultures at different times. These are the elements that are essential to art, wherever and whenever it appears.

Perhaps the major difference between the art of preliterate peoples and our own Western tradition is the reduced connection between art and life in our tradition. In modern Western society it may be true that art "imitates life" and "life imitates art," but we can say this precisely because the two categories are maintained as separate entities. In preliterate societies art reverberates through life. This is most obvious in ritual, and it is for this reason that I have spent so much time in this chapter comparing ritual and theater.

From the perspective of our own culture we define art as nonfunctional ("art for art's sake"), but when we take a comparative view, we must consider its functional role in other societies. Our confusion increases when we discover that many of the world's languages have no word for "art" as a distinct entity. It appears to follow from this that art as a specific category is limited to the Western tradition. But what unites art in all societies is not its functional aspect per se, for this varies both historically and from culture to culture, but rather its gamelike character in which symbolic transformation of formal elements provides the major stimulus for creativity. All art contains information of a special sort that is uniquely packaged and that acts directly upon the subconscious. Our response to art is a unique combination of emotion and subconscious cognitive activity. Art makes the subconscious symbolic system real and objectively present.

Chapter 2

The Evolution of Art

THE CREATION AND appreciation of art in its many forms are uniquely human activities. Yet behaviors as complex as those involved in artistic creativity could not have appeared out of nowhere. In order to discover their origins, let us explore mammalian and human evolution in order to arrive at the biological roots of art.

The hand is a highly specialized organ. Bipedalism and erect posture have freed the human hand for carrying and manipulating objects with a finesse seen only partially in some of our primate cousins. The hand itself is a prehensile (grasping) organ with an opposable thumb. This complex articulation allows us to grasp objects with ease. In combination with rich nerve endings in the fingers, the hand is capable of both a power grip, with which things are firmly held, and a precision grip, which can be used to manipulate small objects with great care. It is this precision grip that allows the production of fine detail seen in much painting and sculpture.

Another evolutionary development important to our over-all adaptation is well-tuned eye-hand co-ordination. The human nervous system is patterned so that what the hand does can be monitored by the eye in great detail. Through complex feedbacks controlled by special brain centers, the hand operates on the basis of instructions formed from visual patterns.

Although more highly developed in primates, flexible limb structure is a primitive characteristic of mammals in general. The stiffness of elephant's legs, for example, is a departure from the original mammalian pattern. The columnar legs of these animals are specializations for the support of great weight. Cats, on the other hand, have retained flexibility in both upper and lower limbs. My own pet cat often sleeps with his paws up over his eyes when the room is brightly lit. He also uses his paws to scoop food out of a dish and carry it to his mouth. This is done, however, only when his food is placed in a deep narrow container against which his whiskers rub when he pushes his face down into it.

Humans have retained limb flexibility in the upper extremities. We have full rotation of the arms and may easily turn our hands over as the radius rotates over the ulna. Flexibility in the lower limbs has been sacrificed somewhat with the development of bipedal locomotion, and, of course, we have lost the use of the primitive primate hand on our feet. Since full bipedalism frees the hand for work, this change was a good trade. Furthermore, with proper exercise a good deal of flexibility is also available in our legs, as manifested in dancers and acrobats.

Our ability to see color and judge distance may be part of our early primate heritage. Humans, like birds, are quite color conscious; other mammals are either color blind or are sensitive to only a small range of what to us is the visible spectrum. The first primates were small insect-eating animals that had to perceive accurately both the distance and the color of their prey as they stalked it in a vegetation-rich environment. Three-dimensional (or stereoscopic) color vision probably continued to be advantageous for tree-dwelling primates, the next stage in the development of our evolutionary line. Stereoscopic vision has an obvious advantage for animals that move rapidly through an aboreal environment, jumping, leaping, and later swinging from limb to limb. Under these circumstances, poor judgment of distance could lead to instant disaster. We need not ponder the selection pressures that favored this trait in evolving primates. Visual acuity, which has implications for the kind of art we produce, evolved with the growth and increasing complexity of the visual centers in the brain.

Yet the olfactory centers responsible for the highly developed sense of smell in such ground-dwelling animals as members of the dog and cat families are much less developed in humans. Primate evolution has seen a decrease in olfaction with an increase in visual acuity. Evolution has traded one set of adaptations for another set under different natural conditions. This process reflects the over-all economy of the selective process.

This is not to say that scents have no part to play in human behavior. Our own culture has both positive and negative associations for particular odors. Food preparation involves both taste and odor, and the perfume industry could not exist if smell were totally unimportant. The same thing is true of some of our negative cultural attitudes about odor. A large segment of our economy is based on products that neutralize our natural smells. Still, our olfactory sense is much less powerful than that of many other species and our ability to recall particular odors when they are absent is quite limited. Most of us can *picture* an object or a person in our mind's eye, but would be hard put to *smell* anything by comparable means. It would be quite surprising if smell were to become a central concern of artists for it occupies only a small place in our symbolism. In fact Shakespeare's poetic line, "That which we call a rose by any other name would smell as sweet," says more about verbal symbolism than it does about pleasant odors. The real subtlety of odors is closed to us. For this reason it was only recently that ethologists turned from the almost exclusive study of visual signals to scents in the analysis of animal communication. We cannot share many of the important odors with other animals and must instead rely on indirect evidence.

The evolutionary developments discussed thus far provide some of the physical and neurological tools for human artistic behavior, but they do not explain why our organs are sometimes used to produce or appreciate art. True artistic behavior is seen in no species other than *Homo sapiens*. Not even a hint of it occurs in the natural behavior of other species. What we do see in the behavior of other animals, however, is a series of traits that provide the necessary precursors for the emergence of art. Each of these can be shown to have a direct selective advantage for evolving mammals in general and primates in particular. Instead of being the direct outcome of evolution, art was made possible by a series of developments that set the stage for its emergence. To understand the place of art in the evolutionary process, therefore, it will be necessary to examine another set of behavioral traits.

The first two of these are exploratory behavior and play. Both are of undoubted selective advantage for species equipped with high learning capacity. Exploration coupled with a high capacity for learning allows an organism to map its environment, while play provides a controlled and protected situation for environmental manipulation. Play is, of course, a widespread characteristic of mammals in general and primates in particular.

We must distinguish between games and play. Play is a more general term referring to any activity that is not directly involved in survival. Games are structured playing. Games have sets of rules that must be known to the players before the game can proceed. Creativity in games is more structured than in free play. Games may have formal structures like chess or cards, or informal structures like playing house or cops-and-robbers. Any play is self-rewarding. One plays for the sake of playing rather than for extrinsic rewards.

All of us are familiar with examples of animal play. Anyone who has had a pet puppy or kitten has seen the play patterns that make up so much of these animals' behavior. Puppies and kittens are fearless as they attack bits of string, shoes, or other objects that can be pushed around or manipulated. Anything that moves is animated and then conquered by them. Cats, at least, later apply this behavior to real hunting. Dogs, as house pets, are restrained in this activity, but those animals used for hunting get a chance to practice their acquired skills. These are sharpened through training, a process that they thoroughly enjoy because, for them, it is just another aspect of play. Baboons and other monkeys are also very playful. Young baboons often play fight, but always under the careful eyes of adults who stand ready to intervene should any of the players emit a cry of pain. Such a signal indicates that the play has become serious.

Omar Khayyam Moore, a sociologist, has suggested that different types of games allow people to learn physical, social, and intellectual skills in a guarded, unthreatening environment.

Moore sees play as a situation in which rewards are self-generated, or, as he puts it, autotelic. This notion has been tested in children as young as three years of age who have been taught to read and write by using an electric typewriter. In his early experiments, Moore seated his subject before an electric typewriter that had been prepared by painting the keys in a range of colors. The child's fingernails were color-coded to match the keys for touch typing. The machine was turned on. Eventually the child would touch a key and a letter would strike the paper. If the key was hit with the appropriate finger, the machine was left on; if not, it was turned off momentarily so that when the child struck another key, there would be no response. After a predetermined period, the machine would be turned on again and another attempt could be made. The experimenter did nothing besides turn the machine on and off. No effort was made to encourage or discourage the child. After the keyboard had been mastered, the experimenter would utter a sound appropriate to a struck letter. In a short time the subjects began to write on the machines and transfer this ability to the reading of texts. The teaching process was eventually automated and the necessary presence of the experimenter eliminated. Under these conditions children were perfectly content to play with the machines and, through play activity, learn to read and write. Rewards were built into the system; the process was completely autotelic.

There is, of course, a difference of degree but not of kind between the adaptive play of young baboons and the controlled experiment described here, but the results are the same. Playing provides an excellent opportunity for learning.

Moore has included art in his discussion of games and has suggested that artistic creation is play activity in which elements of the environment are explored and manipulated with no end other than the play itself. In this way, play and exploratory behavior are intimately connected. Many technological innovations had their origins in art and play. The only evidence of the wheel we have in the pre-Columbian New World, for example, is found in toys.

There is a connection between "word play" and literature, particularly poetry. Writing may be a painful experience even for some professionals, but it is certainly also an autotelic activity, at least for those who write to express themselves. Almost no poets make a living from poetry yet they go on writing it. Poetry involves the exploration of language. It is a game in the sense that it involves a set of rules that act as guidelines to the poetic process. Readers of poetry also enter into this game as they play with a range of possible meanings and emotional qualities built into good poems. Poetry not only exercises our linguistic abilities, it also exercises our unconscious processes leading, in some cases at least, to self-understanding and an enrichment of the personality. Poetry and, in fact, all kinds of literature are kinds of communications games that use language, but are more than just language.

Moore's experiments with game playing and learning illustrate the direct benefit that game playing has for conscious activity. But learning to read and type is not creative in the same sense as reading and writing poetry. Sigmund Freud himself saw artistic behavior as a continuation of and a substitution for the play of childhood. In his 1908 essay "The Relation of the Poet to Day-Dreaming," Freud said the following:

> . . . every child at play behaves like an imaginative writer, in that he creates a world of his own or, more truly, he rearranges the things of his world and orders it in a new way that pleases him better . . .

Now the writer does the same as the child at play; he creates a world of phantasy which he takes very seriously; that is, he invests it with a great deal of affect, while separating it sharply from reality. . . .

. . . when a man of literary talent presents his plays, or relates what we take to be his personal day-dreams, we experience great pleasure arising probably from many sources. How the writer accomplishes this is his innermost secret . . . The writer softens the egotistical character of the day-dream by changes and disguises, and he bribes us by the offer of a purely formal, that is, aesthetic, pleasure in the presentation of his phantasies.

Both Moore and Freud have put their fingers on a different aspect of the relation between game playing and artistic behavior. Few would argue that art springs whole cloth from the conscious mind, and Freud would certainly not have objected to the view that art is a self-rewarding, problem-solving activity as well as fantasy play involving unconscious symbolism.

Play is one biological property that makes art possible in the human species, but culture, not biology, determines a particular tradition and its stability through time. Play as an aspect of art appears in all cultures, but the degree of freedom allowed in the game of art (its formal rules) varies along an art-historical dimension. Egyptian art, for example, changed very little during the many centuries of dynastic rule.[1] Oriental art has

[1] I have always been puzzled by Egyptian art, because of all art traditions, it appears far and away to be the most rigid and least changing. Apparently, individualism did have an outlet, however. In an exchange of views between Gombrich and Quentin Bell published in the spring 1976 issue of *Critical Inquiry* (p. 404), we find the following revelation. Bell writes: "Do you know—but I'm sure you do—those little drawings which they [Egyptian artists] made when they were off duty? . . . They are rapid, expressive, sensitive drawings, drawings by men who could disregard outline and convey all that was needful by the use of accent, scribbles that remind one of Rembrandt—perhaps that's going too far

shown much less formal change than Western art in the same time period. How much freedom an art tradition allows is linked to such cultural factors as the purpose for which works of art are produced (icons, for example, tend to remain very stable), the role of the individual artist in society, and the set of formal rules that surround artistic production. In most cases, no matter how rigid a tradition is, however, there will be some room for individual creativity. In those cultures in which unsigned works are the rule, individual style becomes the mark of particular artists.

Even ordinary game playing involves different degrees of freedom. Game rules, like aesthetic rules, are defined by cultural factors. Chess, for example, has been quite stable for several hundred years although the *art* of playing chess has developed with the individual inputs of a long series of talented chess players.

In eastern New Guinea (now Papua-New Guinea), particularly the Sepik River area and the Gulf of Papua region, a casual look at artistic production (masks, house decorations, and shields) suggests that one major formal principle or rule involves bilateral symmetry along the vertical axis. A close look at objects in museum collections and from photographs taken in the field reveals that in most cases the symmetry is significantly broken. The asymmetrical patterns are so clearly a part of each individual work that it is difficult to imagine that they could occur merely by chance. It is more likely that symmetry is a conventional rule that is meant to be used only as a guideline

---

—but of Tiepolo, of the freest, most perfectly adroit of European hands. . . .

"Perhaps this individual and imaginative art was, as it were, an underground accompaniment to the official art of the Pharaohs, never finding its way into public monuments except during one brief revolutionary epoch during the 18th Dynasty."

by individual artists. If we knew more about creation in these areas, we might be able to develop a means for determining just how particular artists exercise separate styles in the context of an over-all cultural system that sets limits on the outer boundaries of permissible variation. In this and other cases we would then know more about artistic play within the rule system of any artistic game.

The major difference between modern Western art and other traditional art styles lies not in the degree of freedom available to the artist, but rather in the locus of the game itself. In modern art the boundaries of the game extend outward to include a whole set of notions about art and the metaphysics of creativity. Modern art is often "meta-art," that is, it is often a statement about art. Just how the artist plays his or her game is just as important as the material object that is the final outcome of the creative process. This is why it is often so difficult to judge some modern art by traditional standards of craftsmanship.

I have suggested that art is play involving rules and that games are a type of play involving structured rules. Rules imply form. In art, at least, formal rules are reflected in the end product itself. They are frozen in sound or visual space. Even when individual artists vary widely in style, they still conform to some degree to a formal aesthetic system that identifies them as members of particular schools and cultures. Exotic art from alien cultures often arouses interest and appreciation in the West, particularly among artists. Late nineteenth- and early twentieth-century European artists, Pablo Picasso and Georges Braque among them, were inspired by African and Oceanic sculptures exhibited in the Musée de l'Homme in Paris. They saw in these foreign works the same solutions to formal problems that they were dealing with at the time in their own productive activities. Many associate this openness to exotic art with the modern movement, but the sixteenth-century German artist Albrecht Dürer was also impressed by the art of pre-Columbian peoples of Mexico brought to Europe as booty. Could it be that certain elements of form are universal? And if this is the case, are they coded into our brains?

Animal and human studies indicate that many organisms are sensitive to certain spatial configurations. While many of these configurations trigger specific behaviors, such as species recognition or flight reactions (young ducks, for example, will cower when a schematic hawklike image is passed over them), other more diffuse, formal patterns stimulate pleasure reactions. Pictures of immature animals are preferred by adult humans over pictures of mature animals, and babies smile at schematic human faces. Also, several species of monkey and ape will produce formal artlike patterns under laboratory conditions. Such behavior, although artificially stimulated, may reflect brain-based preferences for certain types of spatial arrangement—for what I will describe in Chapter 6 as "good form."

The English naturalist Desmond Morris and other zoologists and psychologists working with various primates have demonstrated that these animals can be stimulated to mark paper with pencil or paint. Interestingly enough, such activity appears to some degree to be ordered. Apes draw fanlike patterns, and after some time and experience with a medium, their "compositions" become more and more complex involving elaborations of the basic design. Color balance may also improve with practice. More significant, however, is the reaction of chimpanzees to a surface marked with squares placed on different parts of an otherwise empty painting surface. When such a square is centered the animal will tend to draw within it, maintaining the centrality of the design. Balancing and inversion also occur. Although some scholars question his methodology, Morris' study shows that when the square is placed on the upper left-hand side of the surface the animal will tend to limit its design to the lower right-hand corner. Placing the square in different corners will elicit responses that conform to this pattern.

More experiments will have to be performed before we can be sure that apes actually can be stimulated to produce designs of this type, but whatever the results, *painting apes are not artists*. Art is a cultural phenomenon involving a whole set of behaviors that we share with other primates, plus another—"transformation-representation," which I will discuss below.

Some mammals other than primates may be acutely aware of spatial relations and the arrangement of units in their environment. Domesticated wolves and coyotes reared as pets in the home become agitated when even small objects are moved away from their habitual positions. This concern for order goes beyond environmental exploration to a coding of familiar surroundings. The agitation generated by changed conditions of the field tends to restimulate environmental exploration and sets the animal on guard against potential danger; thus the adaptive nature of the behavior is obvious.

Humans are, of course, equipped with a highly developed capacity for pattern recognition and discrimination. Such a capacity allows for the storage and coding of a great deal of useful information, including subtle differences in facial patterns which allow unambiguous social discriminations within and among groups. The complex nature of human social interactions is facilitated by this ability. Its operation, however, depends also upon long-term memory storage of complex information, another feature of the human genetic blueprint. Such pattern recognition and discrimination as well as stored memories can be transferred to artistic behavior and the establishment of an artistic tradition.

Nonliterate people are well known among anthropologists for amazing feats of memory. The recently published *All God's Dangers: The Life of Nate Shaw*, by Theodore Rosengarten, illustrates this capacity. Among nonliterate people, encyclopedic information is stored in the minds of the elderly. This knowledge is often organized in the form of myths and sagas, which are passed down from generation to generation. The fact that a good deal of practical information, particularly that relating to social relationships and law, is embedded in myths suggests that these oral literary forms function as structured memory banks. Myths facilitate both storage and recall. The fact that oral literature has both a language and an aesthetic function may also increase its adaptive significance. People need to hear their myths, but they also enjoy hearing them.

Although humans are capable of discriminating and storing a wide range of visual information the accuracy of recall varies with the stimulus. We are able to retain minute details of human facial features much better than architectural and landscape features, although our powers of retention in the latter case are also extraordinary. When it comes to accurately *reproducing* such different configurations as faces or buildings, humans are much more tolerant of deviations or mistakes in buildings than in faces. Slight deviations in portrait drawing change the face. While a person might well still recognize a distorted portrait (this is how we can appreciate and recognize caricatures), deviations will be noted. During the summer of 1975 I did a great deal of drawing in a small village in the South of France. Villagers unhesitatingly recognized and appreciated local scenes. I found it much harder to represent people, particularly faces, and in many cases my portraits were either judged as poor but recognizable, or unrecognizable. I do not think that these differences in reaction can be explained by differences in my own ability to represent. Rather, they were due to a differential tolerance in observers to errors in depicting landscapes and faces. Since facial recognition, so much a part of our social life, depends upon the coding and recall of minute differences, it might well be that both coding and storage mechanisms in the brain act differentially for facial patterns than they do for other patterns.

We do know that pattern recognition, particularly for faces, begins in early infancy. This suggests that innate patterns may have a strong effect on what is learned and how easily it is learned.

Several studies of figure and shape preferences in newborn infants have been published. The results are ambiguous but nonetheless suggest that infants prefer figures of intermediate complexity. This is particularly true when the stimuli contain various angles and curves rather than right angles and squares. This preference may be related to the response that occurs later in child development when an infant will readily smile at a highly schematic drawing of a face.

Evolutionary developments in brain anatomy, particularly the differentiation of speech areas, allowed full language to emerge as a main feature of human behavior.

Human language, as opposed to other forms of communication in lower animals, depends upon the ability to apply arbitrary symbols to objects and concepts and to manipulate these symbols in the context of a grammar to produce thought patterns that can be independent of temporal and environmental elements. That is to say, humans can think backward to

1. New York City subway graffiti of the 1970s. Action painting in popular form.

2. French political poster of 1968 (equating French police with Nazi SS of World War II) showing how the impact of "good form" can carry a verbal message.

3. American lamp (2 feet high), c. 1920. An example of kitsch art in which classical form has been debased by popular form.

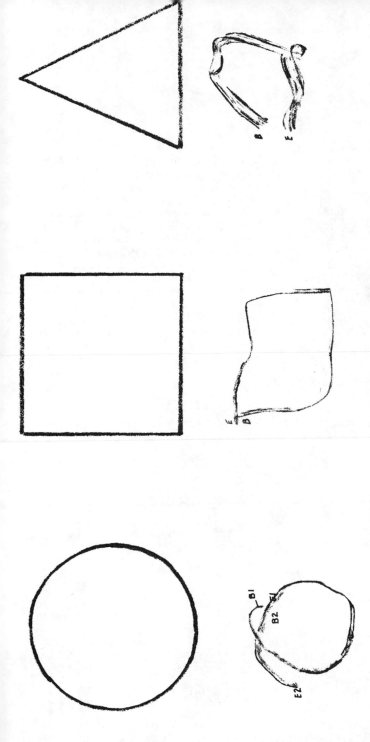

4. In an attempt to test his sense of form, Nim Chimpsky, Columbia University's experimental chimpanzee, was shown a circle, square, and triangle. Underneath these three figures he drew amazingly good replicas of each. The "b" in each figure indicates where Nim started to draw his figure and the "e" indicates where he ended it. It was necessary for him to begin the circle a second time in order for it to approximate the circle he was shown more closely. Nim, a two-and-a-half-year-old male in 1976, enjoyed drawing as much as any human child.

5. Left, Bobo ceremonial mask (wood, 22 inches high), from Upper Volta, West Africa. The abstract face and antelope horns are typical of one conventional style of the Bobo. Variations on this theme can be found among other ethnic groups in the surrounding West African savannah area. The face has been rendered with greater abstraction than the two Baoulé masks in Figures 7 and 8.

6. Below, two Ashanti sculptures from Ghana, West Africa. *Left:* An Akua Ba (fertility) figure (wood, 12 inches high), carried by a pregnant woman to insure the beauty of her child. *Right:* A comb (wood, 10 inches high). Similar stylistic conventions are used in two objects with different uses.

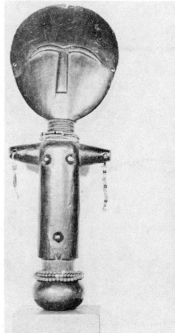

7. Left, Baoulé funeral mask (wood, 14½ inches high), from Ivory Coast, West Africa. The iconography of this mask is distinguished by the small, pouting mouth. The headdress, the shape of the eyes, and the facial scarification are typically Baoulé.

8. Below, Baoulé ceremonial mask (wood, 19 inches high). The author was told that the figure on the top was of the President of Ivory Coast, Felix Houphouët-Boigny. This mask is completely traditional in style. The smiling mouth distinguishes it from a funeral mask (Fig. 7). The clothing on the figure on top illustrates the adaptation of a Western convention to traditional style.

9. Above, sculptural styles from West African ethnic groups. *Clockwise:* Dogon (Mali), Baoulé (Ivory Coast), Babembwe (Zaïre), Yoruba (Nigeria), Ibo (Nigeria). The last, an Ibo ikenga (protective figure) is an example of an abstract but obviously anthropomorphic figure. The others share certain style characteristics (the body proportions, the bent legs) common throughout West Africa. All (from 7½ to 17 inches high) are more or less tubular, reflecting the round logs out of which they are carved.

10. Right, two Dogon sculptures (wood, 13 and 17 inches high) from Mali, West Africa. Both figures are typical of the Dogon style, but the one on the left has better form.

11. Ashanti figure (bronze, about 2 inches high), used as a gold weight from Ghana, West Africa. Small figures like these have greater plasticity than most African wood sculpture. This Ashanti bronze is an inferior piece made for tourists. But enlarged and viewed from the side (*right*), it becomes transformed into an interesting form reminiscent of the Swiss sculptor Alberto Giacometti.

12. Two bronze figures. *Left:* Bes, Egyptian god of women and marriage (9½ inches high), from North Africa. *Right:* A Fon figure (7 inches high), from Benin, West Africa, depicting a man dressed in European clothes; note the powder horn on his head. Both figures are made by the lost-wax process, which allows for a great deal of plasticity. The size of these bronzes permits a greater degree of detail than is found in the much smaller Ashanti bronzes like that in Figure 11.

past events or forward to possible future events. Humans are capable of thinking about and communicating ideas that are reflections of an inner conceptual space. Speech can communicate about the real world and about an imaginary world. We can, for example, think and talk about a three-horned unicorn, as contradictory as this might be. In addition, the meaning of symbols may vary along the dimensions of denotation and connotation, and new combinations of conceptual order may be created and destroyed in the speech-thinking process. Perhaps the essence of linguistic flexibility is contained in metaphor. Metaphors allow us to connect ideas that were previously unconnected. Innovation and creativity both depend upon this ability.

Language allows us to represent ourselves and the world as we perceive them. The cutting away of the symbol from the object or idea represented (the arbitrary nature of the symbol) allows its meaning to be changed. Symbols not only mean but they can be transformed. Since the two processes of representation and transformation are dependent upon each other in the symbolic process I should like to refer to them together as "transformation-representation."

The ability to represent and transform is exclusive to humans. It lies at the base of language as the fully evolved form of human communication. Its appearance in our species is undoubtedly linked to the emergence of language and the kind of social life we lead. Once evolved, however, transformation-representation could serve as the basis for artistic activity as well. The flexibility inherent in language is necessary to its function and to the kind of thinking humans are capable of doing. This flexibility is inherent in our capacity as normal humans to speak, but it is exercised by the playing of language games. Thus our biological capacity for gamelike play and language learning are linked to creativity in both ordinary speaking and literature.

Visual art, dance, and music also involve transformation-representation, because all the art forms are capable of representing our perceptions and deepest feelings. The trick in art, however, is that these perceptions are necessarily represented as transformations. Art requires that they be transformed.

Metaphoric associations as well as other forms of transformation-representation are enhanced by the right hemisphere of the human brain that is known to be associated with musical and visual imagery. (The left hemisphere controls normal speech function.) Damage to the left hemisphere of the brain causes severe speech malfunction. Damage to the right hemisphere impairs an individual's ability to draw and to read visual imagery; in addition, it impairs the ability to handle linguistic images. Howard Gardner, an American psychologist, in his book *The Shattered Mind* notes that while individuals with right-brain damage have no difficulty in understanding the denotation of a particular utterance or word, they lack the ability to appreciate the connotative or metaphorical sense of an utterance:

> For example, asked what is meant by the proverb "Too many cooks spoil the broth," a right hemisphere patient may offer the superficially acceptable response, "What you're cooking won't be good if you have too many people cooking it." Further probing, however, may reveal that he is unable to go beyond this very literal, "concrete" interpretation and to acknowledge that the proverb needn't pertain to food or cooks at all.

Right-brain patients who cannot unravel the meaning of metaphorical statements will tend, however, to talk in puns and jokes. Gardner says, for example, if such a patient is asked what hospital he is in, he might reply "Mount Cyanide Hospital." Here the patient produces an unintentional pun through the connection of word concepts. The difference between metaphorization and pun formation may be the concrete nature of the linguistic material manipulated in the pun as opposed to the rather abstract connections and associations that must be made in metaphor construction. Puns have real and obvious sound associations. They are funny when unexpected, but they are constructed out of literal material. The ability of right-brain-damaged patients to perform transformation-representation is disrupted. The fact that they can't metaphorize and pun unintentionally points to the fact that transformation-representation is a special feature of language and creativity and that it has its own special place in the brain. Gardner compares right-brain-damaged patients to computers. They are capable of decoding what is said to them, but such decoding must be literal. They are stripped of their linguistic imagination and cannot apply a creative interpretation to what is said.

The two parts of the brain provide the common basis for transformation-representation as well as the symbolic flexibility we see in both language and the arts. Human beings, because they have real language (as opposed to even the cleverest ape communication), are capable of extending and limiting meaning at will and in surprising and creative ways. In this sense, human speech is fully open. It can be and is used as the tool for such creative activities as scientific exploration on the one hand and poetry on the other.

While many literary critics believe that there are limits to the openness of symbolic creativity, artists, particularly modern artists, have always managed effectively to question this assumption. Every time painting or the novel is declared "dead," someone comes along to give them new life. The French poet André Breton used to illustrate the openness of creativity by playing a game with his friends called "one-in-the-other." In this game the active player leaves the group and decides upon some image. In his absence the group chooses another. When the player returns the two images are made known. The active player's task in the game is to relate the two images in a short narrative, converting one into the other through the creation of a complex metaphor. Happily we have some notion of the kinds of images that Breton and his friends played with. Roger Caillois, a French psychologist, tells us that Breton's game included the following identifications: a terrier as a flowerpot, a lock of hair as an evening gown, a sorcerer's wand as a butterfly, a leer as a partridge, a shooting gallery as a church proctor, Mme. Sabatier as an elephant's tusk, a pair of sheets as a path, a child being born as an hourglass, a rainbow as the Rue de la Paix, a glowworm as the assassination of the Duc de Guise in 1563, an amazon as a coffee container, a candle as the fourteenth-century scholar Nicolas Flamel making a pilgrimage to Santiago de Compostela.

We have no difficulty in picking out which of these images are easy and which are hard to convert in the process of metaphorization. The ease and difficulty, however, as well as the way such images are made to work will depend upon the structure of a particular language and current cultural associations.

Structure is the "space" through which the imagination roams. Yet the existence of structure means there are limits to creativity and the connectability of symbols. Nevertheless, the symbolic process is completely open and any and all images can be connected. There is no contradiction here. Any image is realizable. What is limited or determined by our culture, as well as by the way the human brain works, are the pathways available to connect images. This does not make creativity finite. There are infinite ways of producing effective metaphors as there are infinite ways of producing an exciting work of art. But it is also possible, and I think likely, that there are an infinite number of dead ends that lead only to failure in the creative process.

Play and exploratory behavior, response to form and the recognition of preference for certain forms over others, fine-grain perceptual discrimination coupled to a high capacity for memory storage, and transformation-representation are all adaptations of our species. The first three are found in many mammals, particularly primates, while the fourth is specifically human. Artistic behavior became possible only with the emergence of transformation-representation, which can readily exploit the other capacities in creative activity.

Once present, artistic behavior can operate as a powerful tool for the exploration of both the environment and the inner space that is ourselves. Artistic creativity adds a new dimension to play and exploration. It makes us more aware of form and it operates as a stimulus to perceptual discrimination. For those who pay attention to art and for those who use it, it is also a tremendous aid in the organization of conceptual material. It can be used to facilitate recall and maintain sets of necessary connections between related bits of information. The formation of information into structures, which is also no doubt a brain function, provides the coherence that underlies both ordinary thought and creativity.

Art may now be defined as play with form producing some aesthetically successful transformation-representation. Art is a kind of autotelic communication game. This, of course, immediately raises a new question: what do I mean by aesthetically successful? I mean that a piece of art that works engenders an

39

emotional response in the creator and, it is hoped, from his or her point of view, in some communicant as well. That is to say, art as a part of communication (semiology) should involve a successful transaction, in this case a communication between the producer of the "signal" and some audience. I agree, therefore, with the American philosopher Susanne Langer that what is communicated in these transactions is the subjective aspect of experience. Art communicates experience that has no direct linguistic signs in spoken language.

This aspect of artistic communication applies to literary as well as other arts because even the verbal arts communicate on a level separate from ordinary discourse. Literature uses words to communicate, but it communicates more than words. It arouses an aesthetic emotion in us. The aesthetic emotion is the response we get when we perform or experience successful art. It is different from the other emotions because it can only be aroused in the context of an aesthetic experience (natural or human-made).

When we look at or hear a work of art that we like, we engage ourselves in a game that the artist has set in motion. We begin the game when our attention is arrested and we feel emotionally aroused. Because art is capable of arresting attention in this way and because it shares certain features with other communication systems, it can be used to carry a specifically linguistic message. This is why so many people confuse art with language rather than recognize that it is one communication game in a family of communication games. The first thing art does is bind our attention. Afterward we may attempt to analyze it. If it has structure, we will tend to think that it must also have a specific intellectual content as well. This is the reason, for example, that we try to give meaning to grammatical sentences that have no meaning. If the rules of grammar are followed, we expect a sentence to have meaning. But what makes art special is the original *nonintellectual* impact it has on an observer.

The seductive aspect of art is biological in origin and is the essence of art. Its force upon a particular individual through the medium of a specific work is, however, constrained by that individual's perceptual and intellectual capacities, personality, and cultural background. Art is rooted in biology and obeys the biological rule that both nature *and* nurture contribute to the realization of its potential in both artists and public.

Let me put the argument another way. Art for biological reasons (which have their roots in separate aspects of mammalian evolution) is capable of arresting attention because it produces an emotional impact which we may properly call aesthetic. What happens after this is purely a cultural question.

Before the invention of writing, art must have had great adaptive significance for the maintenance of social groups. Art is an emotionally charged and culturally central storage device for complex sets of conscious and unconscious information. Structure guards information in well-ordered and easily retrievable forms. It also allows for a certain amount of variation (transformation) without a loss of total information or organization. Transformation is something that is likely to occur by accident, but it is also likely to be part of the aesthetic game in which playing with form is a major element. Transformation without significant changes in over-all structure keeps the game exciting at the same time as essential information is guarded.

The invention of writing no doubt diminished the storage function for art, but the very fact that art can still arrest attention in so powerful a way suggests a continued link between it and the very basis of our emotional and unconscious life.

Chapter 3
The Aesthetic Sense

ALL HUMAN GROUPS have some form of art. Oral literature, myth, and ritual poetry are probably the most widely distributed. These are followed closely by dance and visual art. Sculpture, figures, and masks, as well as ritual costumes, are more common than painting. Outside the West, theater exists primarily in a ritual context although it has recently become secularized, at least in part, in Asia.

An African dancer performing a ritual, a New Guinea wood carver sculpting an ancestor figure, and an American painter working alone and unrecognized in a SoHo studio are worlds apart geographically and culturally, but they have many things in common as well. Those artists who live in preliterate societies produce and manipulate the symbols that maintain their culture's ideological framework. While American artists may no longer join them in this task, artists everywhere strive for self-expression through the playful manipulation of form. The freedom to innovate varies widely, but almost everywhere indi-

43

vidual artists are able to maintain a personal style even as they conform to the sometimes rigid canons of their particular tradition.

Does this mean that there are aesthetic universals in the formal sense? Possibly, but we must not be misled by the fact that art in some form is ubiquitous and that artists everywhere share many of the same goals and attitudes. None of this means that the physical objects or performances that result from artistic activity have any underlying unity. The search for aesthetic universals must focus on the analysis of formal principles and the possible existence of common value judgments about art that cross the barriers of culture.

Very little has been done in the area of formal analysis.[1] In this respect, aesthetics is in very much the same position as linguistics. There are many linguists who are sure that a common universal grammar underlies all languages and all individual grammars. Although they argue cogently for this view and present scattered examples, to date they have been unable to describe such a grammar. Attempts to derive universal, formal, aesthetic rules have also floundered. If they exist, they must be deeply buried under the conventional aspects of style in any culture.

There has been some progress, however, in the area of universal aesthetic judgments, at least in visual art. There is evidence that under the proper conditions individuals in different cultures will express the same preferences when presented with a range of art objects. The first studies, however, were poorly designed or produced negative results.

The search for a universal aesthetic began many years ago

[1] An interesting attempt at formal analysis of music that also deals with the problem of a universal aesthetic is *The Unanswered Question: Six Lectures at Harvard*, by Leonard Bernstein.

with the work of three English psychologists: Dewar, Bert, and Eysenck. Unfortunately their work was marred by a lack of control for cultural factors. All of their subjects were English. Monica Lawlor, also an English psychologist, was among the first to undertake a cross-cultural test of aesthetic preference. She used a set of designs based on common patterns found in West African carving, weaving, and metal work. These were ranked in order of preference by a group of English and West African subjects. Lawlor's results were negative. Although there was considerable agreement within each group of subjects there was no agreement between the English and African groups. In this case, agreement had to be attributed to shared cultural factors.

More recently Irvin Child, a Yale University psychologist who has had considerable experience with cross-cultural material, has reopened the question of universal aesthetic principles. In his early experiments Child gave subjects a set of tests consisting of different perceptual stimuli. These included odorants, hues, color saturation and brightness, polygons, paintings, the so-called Graves test (which involves specially prepared pictures), and the Bully test (which involves samples of recognized art). Subjects exhibited high agreement in preference ratings for simple designs, but this agreement had no consistent relation to any kind of preference for visual art. If the art preferences of a sample drawn from the general public is compared to the preferences of a group of art experts, there is no correlation between them. Aesthetic judgment (as measured by agreement with experts) turns out to be correlated with the amount of formal education in art as well as with experience in looking at art in museums, galleries, books, and magazines. Strangely, it is correlated, *but less so*, with art related activities such as sketching, sculpting, or photography. Such results, of course, once again confirm an educational, and therefore a cultural, role in aesthetic judgment.

Child then decided to see if aesthetic judgment could be related to perceptual and personality factors. He gave his subjects a series of tests in which they had to decipher various forms that were either broken or presented in such a way as to make their accurate reading difficult. These included dotted lines, hidden digits, mutilated words, picture perception with fifteen-second projections, and perceptual relations with a time limit to grasp them so reduced that most subjects would be unable to finish.

There was a consistent tendency for success on this test to be related to aesthetic judgment. Although the statistical significance was low, the result could mean that aesthetic judgment is related to the successful avoidance of incorrect visual perception. Aesthetic sensitivity could, therefore, provide a critical attitude toward visual perception in general. This result intrigues me because it indicates that aesthetic sensitivity is adaptive for humans as one form of visual training. Need I add that it is training with a gamelike aspect.

Three other factors were also strongly tied to aesthetic judgment. Child found a high correlation between such judgment and tolerance of complexity. The ability to notice changes in background stimulation was also closely associated to aesthetic judgment. These included unusual events of any kind. Finally, Child's tests indicated that aesthetic judgment could be related to the avoidance of incorrect visual stimuli. In Child's own words, "a very critical attitude towards one's visual experience may . . . be involved in, or result from, the development of aesthetic sensitivity."

Here again the adaptive value of aesthetic experience is evident, but the argument so far sounds entirely cultural. Aesthetic experience, after all, involves learning in the context of one's own artistic tradition. It is interesting, however, that Child found that the agreement between subjects and the aesthetic judgment of experts is correlated with *independence* of judgment *rather than with conformity*. People don't just learn to like what "experts" like. They and experts agree with each other when they do because of something intrinsic to the stimuli! That is to say, expert judgment appears to be due to some factors *external* to conformity with cultural standards.

Whatever it is that is intrinsic about aesthetic judgments, it is clear that the capacity to make them in conformity with experts must depend upon experience and training. If there is a genetic element in the appreciation of form, it is only activated through the learning process. This, however, is no surprise at all. All biological traits are the result of an interplay between genetics and environment. Organisms are the result of their genes *and* their history. Since humans depend heavily upon learning for survival, we should expect genetic capacities in behavior to be activated only under the influence of culture.

The next step in the process of uncovering aesthetic universals was the testing of experts in different cultures with the same stimuli. If experts constitute the sensitive group, it is only among them that one could expect to find significant agreement across the barriers of culture. Child has been involved in three experiments that test for cross-cultural aesthetic agreement. Child and Leon Siroto, who carried out field work among the Bakwele of the Congo (now Zaïre), showed a sample of photographs of Bakwele masks to a group of Bakwele sculptors and to a group of art history students at Yale who were not familiar with African art. Each group was asked to rank the photos in the sample according to aesthetic value.

While agreement was not absolute, it was significantly high suggesting that aesthetic judgment can be transcultural.

In another study, Child and two colleagues—Clellan Ford and Edwin Prothro—compared aesthetic judgment among Yale University art history graduate students, Fijian natives, and Greeks living in the Cyclades.

One investigator took eleven trios of pictures to the island of Naviti, in Fiji Islands. These were shown to five men and one woman. The men in the sample were competent house builders and also knew how to carve kava bowls and coconut-shell cups. The woman was a skilled mat- and basketmaker as well as a tapa designer.

Subjects were instructed to indicate the order of preference among three pictures in each group. According to the report, they all studied the pictures intently for a time and then made their judgment with no hesitation or wavering. The results obtained show an agreement of 78 per cent, between Fijians and art history students, a truly impressive figure.

The second investigator took five of the same trios used in Fiji to the western Cyclades where they were shown to four local craftsmen who did creative work but who were unfamiliar with the mainstream of Western art. Two were women (a weaver and a painter of ceramics); the other two were men (a potter and a weaver of baskets). The amount of agreement between this group and the New Haven sample was almost as large as the Fijian group (75 per cent as compared to 78 per cent). The sample in this case was so small, however, that the result, while suggestive, is not statistically significant.

The authors note that on the trip to the Cyclades a small sample of the test material was shown to two artists who were familiar with trends in Western art. In this case, the agreement between the Greek judges and the New Haven sample was 86 per cent.

Sumiko Iwao, a Japanese psychologist who worked with Child, compared New Haven experts and a large group of Japanese potters. The largest sample of thirty-six potters was from Tanba, a village where pottery has been made for several centuries. The second group of fourteen potters was from Izushi, a less traditional village. The smallest group, of ten potters, came from the city of Kyoto. The latter were assumed to have the greatest familiarity with Western art.

The stimuli were of two kinds. The first consisted of pairs of black-and-white photographs which measured four by six inches. Each pair represented two works of art of similar type and subject matter. Of each pair one photo had been judged superior by the individual making the original choice of two. These pairs were made into slides and were then shown to fourteen expert judges in New Haven. Only those pairs to which twelve of the fourteen judges agreed with the original ranking were used. Prints of fifty-one of these pairs were then prepared to be used in the cross-cultural test.

The second set of stimuli consisted of pairs of postcard reproductions in color of abstract paintings. There was a 61 per cent agreement for the twelve black-and-white pairs and a 57.5 per cent agreement for the color prints of abstract paintings. Although these correlations may appear low a statistical test showed them to be significant.

In order to test the aesthetic judgment of Japanese experts against American *non*experts, twenty-six of the thirty-six black and white photos used in Japan were shown as projected slides to several hundred suburban New Haven high school students. These subjects were asked to express their aesthetic preference

49

between the two works in each pair. The average agreement between this group of students and the New Haven experts was only 47 per cent while the Japanese experts averaged 63 per cent. In another test a smaller number of these pairs (nine) were used with another group of New Haven high school students. In this case, 57 per cent of the students agreed with the Yale experts. This was still considerably lower than the 68 per cent agreement elicited in Japan from the experts exposed to the same sample group of pictures. Finally, thirty-one of these pairs were shown to Yale College undergraduates. In this case the college students showed a 64 per cent agreement with the New Haven experts instead of the 61 per cent agreement shown by the Japanese potters. The latter result suggests that cultural factors as well as familiarity with art among Yale College students slightly overrode the degree of agreement between art experts in the United States and Japan.

Aesthetic judgment is only marginally related to what we call "taste." An individual who is sensitive to form should be able to rank examples within a particular style even if he or she does not like that style. Taste is undoubtedly a combination of cultural and personal factors that lead an individual to prefer certain styles and dislike others. Most people have probably had the experience of disliking a painting while realizing that it was "well done" or "appropriate" within an unfavored genre. Taste for particular styles is probably also related to the phenomenon of aesthetic fatigue. In our culture, with its imperative for change, styles give way after brief periods of popularity. During the 1930s when the rather severe lines of early modern were favored in furniture and architecture Victorian design was anathema. Art Nouveau, which flourished at the end of the nineteenth century and the beginning of the twentieth, was also out of favor. In the early 1950s, however, both Victorian art and

Art Nouveau experienced a revival and the best work in these styles is now sought after by collectors and museums.

Modern Western art is ruled by convention, one aspect of which, paradoxically, is the desire for rapid change and continuous innovation. As the French anthropologist Claude Lévi-Strauss has suggested, modern art continues to be a code (we think of it as a form of communication) but it has become a code stripped of its referents. Visual art, at least, is cut free from myth and, therefore, to a great extent from structure. Form continues to operate, but the styles in which good form (that which reflects aesthetic universals) is embedded shift rapidly across the art scene.

In those societies in which visual art is still a representation of conscious as well as unconscious symbolism, structure limits conventional change. Visual art cannot stand alone in these cultures. It and what it represents are part of a wider ritual and mythic context. Conservatism is therefore manifested in convention but controlled by structure.

The existence of a genetically based aesthetic response is an interesting discovery, but it tells us little about art as a process. We are still left with questions about art production as opposed to art appreciation. We have practically no knowledge of where the boundaries of artistic creativity lie within our own culture, not to mention other cultures. What it is that makes an artist in any of the art forms also remains a great mystery. This is true even in those cases where we have data on the association of artistic talent within families. In cases where artistic talent appears to run in family lines, it is difficult, if not impossible, to separate out genetic and social factors.

Artistic production particularly in the visual arts appears to be a developmental process. Howard Gardner, in his book *The Arts and Human Development*, suggests that painting and drawing go through stages similar to those indicated for cognitive development by the Swiss psychologist Jean Piaget. Musical talent sometimes appears very early and can develop rapidly in those clear cases of musical genius; the most famous is, of course, Mozart. More normal individuals who go on to become competent musicians must study music for several years before their skills have fully developed. Nonetheless, even in these cases musical ability appears to manifest itself earlier than the other arts. It is not clear why this might be the case, but there is evidence that musical skill is located in a special part of the brain away from both speech and visual centers. In addition, the more mathematical abstract nature of musical talent might mean that it is less dependent on experience than are the other arts. Conversely, writing is most dependent upon experience and apparently develops late relative to other art forms. This is due, no doubt, not only to experiential factors, but also to the orderly development of linguistic and cognitive skills that contribute to the effectiveness of any writer's art.

Even chimpanzee painting and drawing shows development. N. Kohts, a Russian psychologist, in her paper "Infant Ape and Human Child," noted that a chimpanzee that she had studied for three years changed its design patterns. These began with simple lines and evolved toward more complex patterns involving crisscrossing. Desmond Morris' ape, Congo, painted from 1956 to 1959. His pictures became progressively more complex, although in most cases they remained within the framework of the original fan pattern. In the final stage of development, however, Congo did produce circles. As Morris writes:

> Towards the end of his painting career, Congo was producing excellent circles, but nearly always filled them in immediately. Luckily he was filmed at this stage and the careful formation

of a pure circle can be witnessed, followed immediately by a precise filling in of its centre and then finally an overall obliteration.

There is evidence that a great many more people have latent artistic talent than we might suppose from the low frequency of artists within our own culture. The American anthropologist Margaret Mead has pointed out that in Bali the arts are a prime aspect of behavior for all Balinese, and literally everyone makes some contribution to the arts, ranging from dance and music to carving and painting. Nonetheless, an examination of artistic products from Bali shows a wide range of skill and aesthetic quality in artistic production.

Kenneth Koch, a professor of English at Columbia University and a poet, has devoted much time teaching poetry to public school children. His technique involves exposure to examples of good poetry and the assigning of themes familiar to the children. A great deal of freedom of composition is allowed and the results are quite startling. One is impressed with the quality of the poems written, the number of children who write good poetry, and the early age at which a mastery of poetic structure appears.

In the visual arts the Egyptian architect Rameses Wassa Wassef has shown that peasant children with no exposure to art and no experience in artistic production can, under the proper conditions, produce works of amazing force and sophistication. Working in a small village near Cairo, Wassef taught a group of children to weave tapestries. They composed directly on the loom and no cartoons were ever used. The results showed an exceptional freedom of composition which nonetheless in many cases reflected the work of highly skilled artists. Both design and color were highly ordered in the final products. These children were not selected for their talent or disposition. Wassef chose weaving because, while mastering its techniques demands a long apprenticeship, a child can do interesting work from the very beginning. The child is stimulated to conquer the difficulties by the reward of success. The techniques Wassef used in his artistic experiments were similar to those employed by O. K. Moore in teaching children to read and write. In both cases, the exploration was free and autotelic.

Wassef's children differed in formal ability to organize shapes and colors, as well as in ability to represent in a semirealistic way the animals, plants, and humans that so often contributed to the over-all design and content of the finished product. When it comes to realistic art, the ability to represent (to draw accurately from nature) is a talent separate from the ability to compose interesting designs. While many abstract artists are also capable of reproducing or drawing well from nature, they merely choose to do something else in their art, some are only slightly above average in this respect. The American artist Jackson Pollock, for example, was not a very interesting artist until he discovered his particular technique of "action painting."

One sees these distinctions in children's art as well. My own daughter Julie began to show a fine sense of color and design as early as her seventh year. By the age of ten she was producing skilled and complex compositions. Yet she is still less able than some of her peers to copy from nature. Further training might or might not increase her skills in this respect to the point where she will be able to produce aesthetically and formally successful realistic art. I do not mean to suggest that if she develops these skills she will be a better artist.

It is unfortunate that our culture discourages artistic talent of certain kinds. Boys are subject to negative peer-group pressure and sometimes discouraged by adults if they express a desire to dance or write poetry. Art classes in school that stress the coloring of printed drawings or that favor realistic drawing over imaginative compositions tend to blunt creativity.

Although we know little about the limits of artistic creativity, it seems logical to assume that receptivity to art is more widespread (even as a nascent capacity) than the ability to produce art. It takes fewer individuals within a culture to produce and maintain the symbolic order than it takes to preserve it through passive participation or appreciation. Those who do participate in art either as artist or spectator take part in the manipulation of symbols that are derived from convention and animated by aesthetic form and structure. This activity is a significant form of mental exercise characteristic of our species and our species alone. Its roots lie in the mammalian and primate responses to form, but its full flowering is dependent upon the capacity to make and use symbols.

Chapter 4

Art and Information

MR. AND MRS. Smith rarely find themselves in an art museum. On a trip to Washington, D.C., after taking in the usual monuments they wander into the new Joseph H. Hirshhorn Museum and Sculpture Garden. They don't like what they see. Mr. Smith is angered by the lack of definable images and forms in the abstract painting and sculpture. He wants art to mean something. Moments later both he and his wife are particularly offended by a painting by the English artist Francis Bacon in which the meaning is only too clear. For both of them the subject and the manner in which it is represented are ugly. "Art should be beautiful," says Mrs. Smith to her husband. "That's not art," he replies.

Another visitor remarks that he likes the colors and designs of many paintings, but does not know what they mean. He, unlike Mr. Smith, believes that abstract art does have meaning and is moved by the form and color of some paintings. He is, nonetheless, puzzled and offended by his inability to make verbal sense out of much of the work he sees. If the artist were present, he would ask, perhaps a bit aggressively, for an explanation.

Artists themselves are notorious for their unwillingness to explain their works. Many will say that a painting explains itself or, as the American poet Archibald MacLeish once said, "A poem should not mean but be." Occasionally this silence is partially broken. Calvin Tomkins reports the following account by Robert Rauschenberg of a conversation he had with an elderly lady who asked the artist why he painted ugly things:

> "Well I had to find out first of all what she meant by 'ugly,' and so we talked about that for a while, and it seemed that what bothered her was the materials I'd chosen to use, and the way they were put together. To her, all my decisions seemed absolutely arbitrary—as though I could just as well have selected anything at all—and therefore there was no meaning, and that made it ugly. So I told her that if I were to describe the way she was dressed, it might sound very much like what she'd been saying. For instance, she had feathers on her head . . . And around her neck she had on what she would call mink but what could also be described as the skin of a dead animal. Well, at first she was a little offended by this, I think, but then later she came back and said she was beginning to understand. She was really serious about it, and intelligent. The thing was, she just hadn't been able to *look* at the pictures until somebody helped her."

"Arbitrary" meant "ugly." This woman wanted to understand the principles behind the choice of materials and construction of Rauschenberg's paintings. For her, as for many, art is the opposite of randomness. It is a manifestation of inspired organization. Art takes its special qualities from this organization and even its meaning. The beauty and "sense" in art

58

come from a rational choice of materials and subject matter as well controlled execution. These factors add up to the form and content of a work of art. When people are familiar with a culture-wide symbolic system, they do not question the ways in which these symbols are represented; therefore nothing is arbitrary. In our society, on the other hand, particular styles are far from universally accepted. The means by which these styles are represented may be understood by only a few. To everyone else the means are arbitrary and the art meaningless.

Every member of all the world's cultures speaks and understands the language of that culture. Every member of every nonliterate culture in the world also understands and responds to that culture's *public* art. (There are cases in which certain art forms are intentionally esoteric and which exclude certain categories of people from the initiated.) Not every member of modern Western society understands modern Western art nor is sensitive to it aesthetically. This is the result of a process in which art has become a peripheral phenomenon in our culture. Art is no longer important to the public at large, but only to artists and their specialized public.

Nonetheless, many people still see art as a kind of language. It would be more correct to say, however, that the tendency to equate art and language rests on metaphor. But even if this is so, what makes this metaphor possible? What are the points of similarity between art and language? This question is complicated by the existence of different schools within the same artistic medium and by the existence of several "arts" in different media. Some authors talk about art, but only mean plastic art, while others attempt to include all art forms.

First of all we must make a clear distinction between communication and language. Communication is a process that is widespread in nature. It involves a sender who transmits a message through some medium (or channel) to a receiver who decodes the message. Communication is a means of transferring a message from one organism to another. A message may be transmitted within and even between species. Plants, for example, by the color and form of their flowers, send messages to bees, birds, and other organisms who, responding to a food signal, fertilize the plant. Humans communicate their presence to mosquitoes by exhaling carbon dioxide into the air. In the first case, the communication aids the sender of the signal. In the latter case, it aids the receiver. Communication among members of the same species may have a greater resemblance to what we conceive of as language because the messages sent often (but not always) involve the auditory channel, and because the signal system is two-way, a receiver can become a sender and vice versa. While these traits are indeed characteristic of human language, they are not the only ones that make our communication system unique. Human speech is highly flexible. An infinite number of sentences can be generated dealing with any idea that we might wish to express. These are communicated through the use of a restricted number of sounds that in combination generate words linked according to specific rules into grammatical utterances. The meanings of particular words may be expanded or contracted to emphasize their connotative or denotative sense and these meanings may change rapidly through time. While animal communication involves immediate stimulation (what is signaled—danger or food, for example—must actually be present), humans can talk about what happened yesterday, what might happen tomorrow, or even about totally imaginary things.

Language is not without ambiguity. If it were a totally unambiguous system, we would need no lawyers or literary critics, but it would also lack the flexibility that makes it so useful in adapting to new situations. As ambiguous as language is, however, it is a far better communication system than art. When art signifies unambiguously, it does so because the code used stands for, and can be translated into, words. The art of comic strips accompanied by a text is very low in ambiguity. Advertising art is like comic strip art in this respect, but good advertising carries multiple messages some of which are perceived only on the unconscious level. Clever advertisements speak on the conscious level, but also arouse emotions on an unconscious level. When art communicates in this way, it has been converted into a code for language messages much as the Morse code employs nonlinguistic sounds, lights, or signs that are converted or translated into ordinary language. The fact that art communicates as well as the fact that it may, under certain circumstances, be used as a linguistic code leads us to the metaphoric use of language for art.

Like language, art is a transactional activity between sender and receiver involving messages. Artists do indeed attempt to express something with their art. The observer sensitive to a work of art receives a message and attempts to decode it, with, it must be added, different degrees of success. Art belongs to a communications family containing ordinary language and other semiotic forms. (The term "semiotic" to cover all forms of communication was used by the Swiss linguist Ferdinand de Saussure.)

Art is semiotic in two ways. The first is the cultural function already discussed. Art, like other cultural elements, can, but need not, carry a linguistic message. The second way is more general, involving a basic characteristic that art shares with language. All art, whether it is realistic, representational, or abstract, involves some form of implicit or explicit symbolism. Even pure abstractions are symbolic. They convey moods and harmonies. In addition, art, like language, involves transformations that are both internal (its grammatical aspects) and external (its relationships to what it represents or symbolizes).

The relationship between art and language is based on the underlying fact that, like any communicative device, art is expressive and, like language, has structure that is probably something like grammar. We know much about the grammar of music, quite a bit about the grammar of poetry, a little about the grammar of dance, and almost nothing about the grammar of the visual arts. Arts that are strung out in time (literature, dance, music, and the mixed-form theater) are easier to analyze grammatically, for the simple reason that they are made up of sequential events. We can tell what direction things go in, and we know where to start and to stop. We can look for recurring regularities in these sequences and derive rules for their occurrence.

Visual art, as Susanne Langer has pointed out, is there all at once. We know very little about the rules for reading it. (I do not mean here rules for reading such technical aspects of art as, for example, perspective.) We are, I am afraid, still in the uncomfortable position of not knowing whether a painting is to be taken as a symbol or a set of symbols or in what sense both of these might be correct.

There are two basic communication channels employed in the arts. These are the visual and the auditory. The art forms that fall within each of these channels share an important element, but they can also be separated on the basis of other qualities. Music and the verbal arts both use sound, but only one employs language. One may, of course, put words to music, but such a combination produces a mixed art form. The spatial arts—dance on the one hand and painting and sculpture on the other—can be separated on the basis of their temporal and non-temporal elements. Dance like auditory arts unfolds through time, while painting and sculpture are there all at once. The fact that dance may be done to music or to words, or both, for that matter, does not make it an auditory art, for its primary impact is visual. Theater, on the other hand, is a true mixed form that can employ each of the other arts in various combinations. The use of space, time, and sound with or without words give the various arts their particular qualities and locate them in relation to language. Because the temporal arts proceed through time, their structure can be grammarlike and rules can be derived for the unfolding process. The verbal arts, for obvious reasons, must have rules that closely overlap the grammar of ordinary speech, while dance may follow a set of kinesthetic imperatives along with a narrative structure if it also tells a story. Painting and sculpture will also be regulated by some set of rules, but since the elements of these art forms occur together, all at once, the rules that govern them will be less like a language grammar.

Our response to the visual arts also may be controlled by a different part of the brain than that which controls speech function. Music, although it proceeds through time, has its own brain centers as well.

As we have already seen, art communicates because, like language, it is expressive form. The affinity does not end here, however, for just as words can be used artistically, art *can* be and frequently *is* used verbally. As I have already pointed out, art may carry a specifically linguistic message. Nonetheless, because the essence of art is different from that of ordinary speech, it is important to distinguish between two different types of information that can be communicated. These are *semantic* and *aesthetic*. Semantic information is contained in language as well as in other forms of communication, such as the call systems of apes and monkeys. It is also contained in art. Aesthetic information is peculiar to that which we perceive as art.

Aesthetic information can be contained in works of art that have a manifestly ugly content. If we can show that this is so, we shall be forced to evoke something other than content (structure or form, for example) as the locus of aesthetic information. We shall be forced to admit that the aesthetic is reflected in the way that information is organized.

Let me bring this discussion down to earth by offering an example of successful art that deals with a conventionally ugly subject. What follows is a description of seasickness drawn from *Death on the Installment Plan* (*Mort à crédit*), by the French author Louis-Ferdinand Céline.

> My mother took refuge in the shelter where the life jackets were kept . . . She was the first to vomit across the deck and down into third class . . . For a moment she had the whole area to herself. . . .
>
> Some of the others began straining their guts over the side . . . In the rolling and pitching, people were throwing up any old place, without formality . . . There was only one toilet . . . in one corner of the deck . . . It was already occupied by four vomiters in a state of collapse, wedged in tight . . . The sea was getting steadily rougher . . . At every rising wave, oops . . . In the trough a dozen oopses, more copious, more compact . . . The gale blew my mother's veil away . . . It landed wringing wet on the mouth of a lady at the other end . . . who was retching desperately . . . All resistance had been abandoned. The horizon was littered with jam . . . salad . . . chicken . . . coffee . . . the whole slobgullion . . . it all came up . . .
>
> My mother was down on her knees on the deck . . .

she smiled with a sublime effort, she was drooling at the mouth . . .

"You see," she says to me in the middle of the terrible plummeting . . . "You see, Ferdinand, you still have some of that tuna fish on your stomach too . . ." We try again in unison. Bouah! and another bouah! . . . She was mistaken, it was the pancakes . . . With a little more effort I think I could bring up French fries . . . if I emptied all my guts out on deck . . . I try . . . I struggle . . . I push like mad . . . A fierce wave beats down on the rail, smacks against the deck, rises, gushes, rolls back, sweeps the steerage . . . The foam stirs up the garbage and spins it around between us . . . We swallow some of it . . . We spit it up again . . . At every plunge the soul flies away . . . At every rise you recapture it in a wave of mucus and stink . . . It comes dripping from your nose all salty. This is too much! . . . One passenger begs for mercy . . . He cries out to high heaven that he's empty . . . He strains his guts . . . And a raspberry comes up after all! . . . He examines it, goggle-eyed with horror . . . Now he really has nothing left! . . . He wishes he could vomit out his two eyes . . . He tries, he tries hard . . . He braces himself against the mast . . . he's trying to drive them out of their sockets . . . Mama collapses against the rail . . . She vomits herself up again, all she's got . . . A carrot comes up . . . a piece of fat . . . and the whole tail of a mullet.

Certainly anyone who has suffered extreme seasickness can appreciate this selection, which distills the horror and misery of the experience. The compactness of the description renders it poetic; it becomes an exaltation of involuntary physical effort, an apotheosis of degradation. To call it a "beautiful work" in the ordinary sense, however, would be to stretch a metaphor beyond recognition. Clearly the quotation arouses our empathy, but seasickness is a tricky subject. A clumsy description could merely make us queasy. We are captured in this case by the movement and structure of the text as well as the rapid juxtaposition of images: banal versus sacred, particular versus universal, serious versus humorous.

Works like *Death on the Installment Plan* force us to admit that semantic information is not the source of artistic merit or aesthetic satisfaction. Such works also force us to explain how art works aesthetically, that is to say, how it imposes its emotional impact on us. The problem of aesthetic information has been approached by Abraham Moles in his book *Théorie de l'information et perception esthétique*. It is from Moles that I have borrowed the concepts of semantic and aesthetic information, but before I distinguish them it might be useful to summarize those aspects of information theory in general that are germane for our discussion of art.

Information theory concerns the analysis of messages of any type. These can be, for example, the messages contained in the genetic code, or the information in the sentence of a particular language, or the same information translated into some artificial code. All messages require: a sender; a signal of a certain type; a medium or channel through which the signal is transmitted; and a receiver. For a message to be received and decoded, it must occur above a certain threshold of loudness, brightness, et cetera. The receiver must be able to distinguish differences between signals—through change in pitch, length of signal, or intensity, for example. In addition, signals must persist long enough to be consciously perceived; too short a signal may go unnoticed. Obviously, all of these factors interact with each other so that a change in one will influence the effectiveness of the others. A short soft tone may go unnoticed while the same sound level played over a longer period may be easily perceived. A short flash of dim light may go unnoticed while a longer flash of the same intensity may attract attention.

In order to understand information theory it will be necessary to discard any notions you might have about the equivalence of information and meaning. Strange as it may seem, information is a function of novelty and not of sense. Confusion over this matter when it occurs probably arises from a nontechnical or "common sense" definition of information.

A message with the highest possible amount of information is one that *must* contain only new and unpredictable elements. If you can predict something in advance, it is not "news" and therefore it is not information. Thus a sequence of random letters (ARWOLHHGGGOWWDSAP) contains more information than the perfectly good sentence, "The dog bit the man." This is because in the case of random letters the receiver cannot predict in advance any of the letters on the basis of preceding parts of the message. If you have already seen or heard ARWOL you will have no way of knowing or predicting that HHGGG will follow. To take another example, there is more information in a series of random numbers than in a set that increases by threes. Once you have guessed that the series is orderly, you will be able to predict the next number. Thus if you are presented with 3, 6, 9, 12 . . . you will predict that the next number will be 15. Since you already know the number will be 15, when it arrives no new information will be added to the message.

In the case of the sentence, "The dog bit the man," the probability of the letter *e* following the initial *th* is very high. If you can predict its occurrence, it does not add information to the message. In addition, the use of the word *the*, which occurs twice in the sentence, is unnecessary; that is to say, it adds no information to the sentence. "Dog bit man" conveys the same information as "The dog bit the man."

Information is different from significance and independent of it. These two concepts must be separated because they have different functions in messages. When they are combined and confused, we cannot sort out the way in which messages work.

Because the highest amount of information (unexpectedness) is contained in a random and therefore unpredictable series of signals, intelligibility (and therefore significance) varies inversely with information. For a message to be intelligible, it must meet a series of expectations.

For a message to be intelligible, it must contain a certain amount of redundancy. (A series of random letters contains no redundancy but it is also unintelligible.) A message with maximum information has no form. It cannot be organized and therefore cannot be read. Such a message has neither significance nor aesthetic form. But a message with too much redundancy will be banal. It will be intelligible, perhaps overly so, and will therefore have little significance. It will also have very little aesthetic value. This is not to say that the surface content of great literature is not sometimes banal. Poems about love and death abound and we are not surprised when they occur. Good poems on these subjects, however, express ideas in an original and somewhat unpredictable way. In this sense, they are high in information. Information theory provides us with the following set of opposed pairs:

> Predictable——Unpredictable
> Intelligible——Informative
> Banal——Original

Moles suggests that there are two forms of information, semantic and aesthetic. The same page of symbols—a page of text in an ordinary book, for example—possesses a different repertoire for individuals with different interests and training.

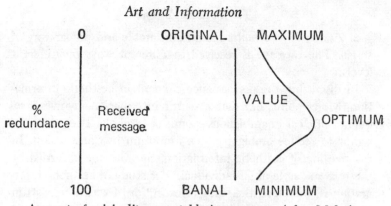

Art and Information

0   ORIGINAL   MAXIMUM

%   Received   VALUE
redundancy   message   OPTIMUM

100   BANAL   MINIMUM

Amount of originality acceptable in a message (after Moles).

Each person finds redundancies and originality in a work. These are functions of knowledge, mental habits, et cetera. In artistic messages, each individual possesses a set of understandings, personal and cultural, that determine the information received. If the perceiver possesses an integral understanding and expectation of all the characters of the message, information is nil and redundancy is 100 per cent. The message, in these cases, is without interest; it is banal. But is this really the case for art? Why then reread or recite a poem we know well? Our interest will be maintained for a long time if there is a reservoir of originality in the work. Originality is never unextinguishable.

But how can art carry such a reservoir of originality? The answer is that it carries complex multiple messages with multiple connections and structures. In addition, different interpretations by both performer and perceiver emphasize different aspects of an art work; the meaning is never fixed. Semantic information and aesthetic information, therefore, contrast as follows:

1. *Semantic information* is logical, structured, expressible, translatable, and preparatory of actions.

69

2. *Aesthetic information* is untranslatable and preparatory of states. The message is received in different ways on different levels.

In discussing the performance element in aesthetic information, Moles points out that semantic information involves a sequence of clear unambiguous sounds or symbols. There is an attempt to reduce ambiguity to a minimum in transmission. In the sending of aesthetic information, the message is carried by the text *and* style of an individual. The study of aesthetic information is, therefore, the study of execution. Execution exists in the text as such, for the text expresses an artist's particular way of shaping a message. Execution also exists in the performance of a text as in a reading of prose or poetry, playing music, dancing, and so on. In the last case, the performer interprets the original text.

Aesthetic information is determined partially by chance and is specific to the sender and the receptor. It varies according to individual knowledge and a multiple series of associations that individuals make among symbols. For this reason, it is a difficult concept to understand and measure. This is a major reason why aesthetic works are so difficult to analyze, but it is also the source of richness in art. The relation between signified and signifier, the object and its sign, is never closed. Multiple interpretations are always possible. In music and also in theater and poetry read aloud, signals possess great liberty in rapport with the semantic message. The same message can be sent (performed) in many ways. This is the interpretive aspect of the aesthetic code. The way in which a work is interpreted opens up new associations and therefore changes in emotional, aesthetic, and even semantic impact.

Poems are sound messages even when they are written down. The value of a poem comes from its being and not its function.

It comes from the interaction between form and significance. Poetry is a mixed form, borrowing rhythm, assonance, repetition, and timbre from music and the telling of something from discourse. As with music, the aesthetic aspect rests on the sequence of variations which cannot be normalized and which play within the coded message itself.

The distinction between aesthetic and semantic information touches upon the frequently raised problem of form versus content in art. Semantic information is the content (message) of a work. Aesthetic information is derived from form—the way a piece of music is constructed and played, for example. This said, it must also be emphasized that both form and content are inseparable parts of the same work. Content is expressed in form, and formal elements affect the way in which content is perceived and interpreted. Furthermore, aesthetic information can only exist as the unique expression of formal elements in particular combinations. This is precisely why a work of art cannot be translated and remain unchanged.

The way aesthetic information operates in great works of art can be intuited from such expressions as, "We constantly see new things in great art," or, "We hear new things in great music that well up from the depths of its structure."

The degree of information in a work, however, depends upon the sophistication of the viewer or auditor. What is noise for one may be music for another. What is redundant for one may be innovative for another. In addition, if we are offended by the subject matter or form of a work of art, as were Mr. and Mrs. Smith in the Hirshhorn Museum, we are unlikely to make any interpretive effort at all. Our aesthetic sensibility will be blocked. It is for these reasons that the aesthetic response is a very personal matter. Artistic appreciation comes from experience and desire as well as from the ability to decipher aesthetic messages and to appreciate their form. In this sense, the aesthetic response is acquired behavior. The fact that humans can experience art as art, however, suggests that the response is based on innate potentialities. The capacity for aesthetic sensitivity must be built into the human species.

Chapter 5

The Structure of Art

To ASK WHAT Shakespeare meant in *Hamlet* is to raise an important but a false question. It is important because it forces us to probe the play for meaning. Such probing enhances our appreciation of the play. It is a false question because the greatness of *Hamlet* comes from the *multiple* possibilities and ambiguities inherent in the text. Yet not all ambiguities are interesting nor are they art. *Hamlet* is great art because it plays upon our aesthetic sense.

Shakespeare loads his plays with aesthetic information. All interesting works of art contain a high degree of aesthetic density. This density is organized rather than chaotic. Remember, information must have structure to be significant. Structure is like the steelwork of a skyscraper. It is hidden under the surface of cement and glass, but it supports the entire work. To know how and why a building stands we must probe its structure.

Structure is a property of all sensual experience. Without it, our perceptions would lack coherence. We would, for example,

The Artistic Animal

see no form without structure, but only a blaze of light. All
sense data is filtered in our brains and organized by mental networks. These networks are genetic in origin, but are only
formed through experience. We shape our world by experienc-
ing it. In order to work, our faculty for organization must be
exercised.

Aesthetic experience is a complex game in which our senses
play with structure. Structure is inherent in a work of art. Our
minds react to it, play with it, often unconsciously. It is not
usually apparent, but it is always there providing the coherence
necessary for significance.

Certain kinds of structure are more likely than others to bind
our attention. Our brains are programmed to work in specific
ways and all human experience shares certain commonalities.
Aesthetic experience is a heightened form of structural experience in which the imagination roams through a structured
space. Even though this space has a set of givens, a set of finite
paths, it may be explored in an almost infinite number of ways.

One feature of literature, according to Lévi-Strauss, the
founder of structural anthropology, is that it is built out of a
structure of oppositions and contradictions. These are mediated
by special devices or characters in the story. The English anthropologist Mary Douglas has suggested that the mediator will
often be a creature that is in some sense anomalous within a
particular cultural context. Certain animals are likely candi-
dates for this role. Douglas notes, for example, that in South
Asia the pangolin is often the chosen mediator. The pangolin is
a mammal that is covered with scales like a fish. Although it is
slow and clumsy, it climbs trees; a strange beast indeed! Anomalous creatures function as mediators specifically because they
overlap conceptual categories. In order to function well,
classification systems must be constructed out of discrete seg-

74

ments with clear boundaries. But all such systems are impositions on nature, which does not always fit into neat boxes. It is the leftover, overlapping natural units that are anomalous, and it is the anomalies that, by virtue of their ambiguity, can be mobilized to join contrasting sets and mediate their ideological contradictions. It is not difficult to see why the pangolin, a rather outlandish creature, might be used as a mediator. In other cases the anomaly may be less obvious. It might be the artifact of the classification system itself. Howsoever people classify nature, creatures are bound to exist that do not fit into the units of an established system. Let us see how this works in a simple folk tale I collected among the Abron of the Ivory Coast.

HOW MAN GOT SORES

Once long ago a spider was wandering through the forest when it heard a woman singing. The song pleased the spider very much and it began to look for the woman. The spider followed the sound until it came upon her. After greeting the woman, the spider said: "I like your song very much." "Would you like to learn it?" asked the woman. "Yes," replied the spider. "Then you must do what I do and repeat the song as I sing it," said the woman. The woman danced and sang her song. The spider imitated her movements and sang along with her. As it did so, the sores which covered the woman's body began to heal and little by little they appeared on the spider's body and legs. When her sores had completely healed, the woman stopped singing and dancing, but the spider could not stop for it was crying and dancing in pain. The woman went back into the forest and the spider continued on its way. Soon it came to a village of men. When they heard the spider's song, the people of the village came out to greet it. After they had exchanged greetings, the spider asked the villagers if they would like to learn its song. "Yes," replied

75

the villagers. "It is very beautiful." "Then you must all do as I do and repeat the song as I sing it," said the spider. The spider danced and sang its song. The villagers imitated the spider's movements and sang along with it. As they did so the sores on the spider's body and legs began to heal and little by little they appeared on the bodies and legs of the villagers. When the transformation was complete the spider said, "Thank you," and disappeared into the forest. This is how man got sores.

This is, of course, a "just so" tale of the type familiar to many in the folklore of the American South. The punch line is almost a letdown in the context of the action. An analysis suggests, however, that the story is a bit more complicated and interesting than might appear on the surface.

In this story the spider is the mediator between culture and nature, between the human world and the world of the untamed. Spiders fit this position well since they live both in the forest (in nature) and in villages (among people). In the context of West African technology, spiders cross the barrier between nature and culture in another way. The spider spins thread and weaves. An animal, a creature of nature, performs a cultural act *naturally*.

The spider walks through the forest and hears a woman. (A human, but not part of the cultural world. She is located in the forest, according to the fable, and does not appear to have any connection with the villagers who have not yet received sores.) The spider gets sores through a fault of communication. It confuses the woman's writhing and crying in pain, which falls in the realm of nature, with a cultural act: singing and dancing. The spider is tricked and wanders off again through the forest until it comes to a village. Here it intersects the cultural world. The same fault of communication—this time the mistake is on the part of humans—leads to another transfer across the boundary of nature and culture. The spider is cured and henceforth human beings are afflicted with sores.

The tale does not produce a resolution of conflict or contradiction. It marks, rather, the dire consequences that can occur when the boundaries between nature and culture are breached. That this is a real concern among the Abron is borne out by other cultural facts. For example, before land is cultivated, religious sacrifice must occur. Abron see this act as an apology to the land for breaking the natural order. In addition, individuals who farm on the Abron holy day are attacked by bush devils and either disappear into the bush forever or return to the village in a state of madness. (They act like animals.) Furthermore, all Abron fear witches who are believed to be both human and supernatural, that is, both cultural and natural. In Abron cosmology there is no break between the natural and supernatural order. Witches can change themselves into animals and, like European witches, are said to work in consort with animal familiars. The spider tale is a secular means of reinforcing the notion that a separation between the domains of nature and culture is necessary to maintain order.

Let us now examine a more complex example. It is a version of the Cinderella tale collected from European folklore.

There was once a schoolmistress who was also a widow. She had a daughter who was very plain. She also had a pupil, Cinderella, the daughter of a traveler, who was very pretty. The mistress was in love with this girl's father. She often begged the girl to convince the father to marry her. If the girl succeeded, the mistress promised that she would give the girl porridge made with honey. The father told his daughter that if he married the mistress, the mistress would give her porridge made with gall. The girl did not believe her father and, crying,

77

begged him to marry the mistress. Because he loved his daughter very much and wanted to satisfy her, the father finally said he would marry the mistress when a pair of iron boots he hung up on the house rusted to pieces with age. His daughter was very pleased to hear this and ran to tell the mistress. The mistress then instructed the girl to wet the boots with water every day and soon they fell to pieces. When this happened, the girl ran to tell her father and he agreed to marry the mistress. Just so long as the father was at home his daughter was treated by the mistress with kindness and affection, but the minute he went out she was treated cruelly.

One day the mistress sent Cinderella out to graze a cow. She gave the girl a loaf of bread, which she was to bring back whole, and an earthen pot of water out of which the girl was expected to drink, but which she was to bring back full. Another day the mistress asked the girl to wind some skeins of thread until evening. The girl left the house crying and bewailing her lot, but the cow comforted her. The cow told the girl not to be distressed but to fix the skein on its horns and simply wind the thread as it unraveled. After that, the good cow took all the crumbs out of the loaf by making a small hole in it with one of its horns. The cow then stopped up the hole so that the girl could give the loaf back whole. In the evening the girl returned home with all of her work done, carrying the whole loaf and the full water pot. The mistress was very angry. She said that she was sure that the cow had helped the girl and ordered that it be killed. The girl was ordered to clean the cow's entrails in a tank of water. Before it died, the cow told the girl not to grieve, but to do as the woman told her. In addition, the cow told the girl to save whatever she saw come out of the entrails. The girl did as she was told and when she was cleaning the entrails she saw a ball of gold come out of them and fall into the water. The girl went down into the tank to search for it.

The girl went into the tank to search for the ball of gold and there she saw a house with everything in disorder. She began to arrange it and soon the house looked tidy. Suddenly she heard footsteps and hid herself behind the door. Some fairies entered and began to look about. A dog who came in with them said: "Bowwow! Behind the door hides somebody who did us good and will render us more services." The fairies searched about and found the girl. They led her out, saying: "We endow you by our powers with the gift of beauty, making you the most lovely maiden ever seen. We cast a sweet spell over you, so that when you open your mouth to speak, pearls and gold shall drop from your lips. We endow you with every blessing, making you the happiest maiden in the world. Take this wand, it will grant your every request." The girl then left the enchanted region and returned home. As soon as the mistress's daughter saw her, she cried out for her mother to come quickly and see "the hearth cat." The mistress asked her what she had been doing all the time she was absent and the girl, following instructions given to her by the fairies, told her the opposite of all that had occurred. She said that she had found a tidy house and had disarranged everything in it to make it look untidy. The mistress then sent her daughter into the tank. No sooner had she arrived there than she began at once to do what her stepsister had told her to do. Soon the house was very untidy. When she heard the fairies coming she hid behind the door. The little dog saw her and began to bark. "Bowwow!" it said. "Behind the door stands one who has done us much harm and will continue to molest us." The fairies, hearing this, approached her and said, "We throw a spell over you which will render you the ugliest maid that can be found. We bewitch you, so that when you attempt to speak, all manner of filth shall fall out of your mouth. We bewitch you and you shall become the poorest and most wretched maid that ever lived." The mistress's daughter returned home thinking that she looked beautiful, but when she came to her mother and began to speak, the woman burst into tears. Full of rage, she turned on her stepdaughter and sent her to the kitchen saying that she was nothing but the hearth cat, and that she should remain there as that was the only place fit for her.

One day the mistress and her daughter went to the races. Cinderella was left at home, but as soon as mother and daughter were out of sight she asked her magic wand to grant her a beautiful dress, boots, a hat, and everything else she needed to be elegant. She dressed herself and went to the races. Once there, she stood in front of the royal box. The mistress's daughter spied her and cried out to her mother that the beautiful girl near the royal box was their very own Cinderella. The mother replied that it could not be true because Cinderella had been left at home under lock and key. When the two women returned home, they found Cinderella dressed in rags with ashes on her face. When asked if she had been out, she replied that she had been in the house all day.

Meanwhile the King, who had seen Cinderella standing before his box at the races, fell in love with her.

For two more days, the mother and daughter went to the races leaving Cinderella at home. Each time she asked her magic wand to provide her with beautiful clothes and each time she went to the races where she stood before the royal box. The King's love for her grew stronger each day, but after the races Cinderella ran in haste to her carriage and disappeared. On the last day, in her haste, Cinderella let fall one of her slippers. The King picked it up and, returning to the palace, fell lovesick. The slipper had some letters on it which said, "This shoe will only fit its owner." The King sent messengers throughout the kingdom with the shoe, trying it on all the women they could find. The schoolmistress went to the palace to try the slipper on but it would not fit. Her daughter followed, but without success. The King inquired who was the next to try on the slipper and asked the mistress if there was any other woman left in her house who could try on the slipper. The schoolmistress replied that there was only the maid Cinderella, but that she had never worn such a slipper. The King ordered Cinderella to be brought to the palace and insisted that he himself try to put the slipper on the girl. The moment Cinderella put her little foot into the slipper and drew it on, it fitted exactly. The King then arranged that she should remain in the palace and soon they were married. He ordered that the mistress and her daughter be put to death.

We are confronted with an initial series of contrasts and oppositions. The story begins with a woman without a husband and a man without a wife. Each of them has a daughter, one plain, the other pretty. The woman wants to marry the man; the man resists. The woman uses the man's daughter to get the man. The agent of her success is a pair of iron boots that in principle should prevent the marriage. Through the actions of the mistress, they fall apart and allow the marriage. The mistress promises her stepdaughter porridge made with honey. Her father realizes that she will only get porridge made with gall (bitter for sweet). The tale leaves out difficulties between the man and his wife. In the beginning it deals with the relations between two generations actualized by the marriage.

The negative relationship between the stepmother and the girl contrasts with the positive relationship between the girl and the magical cow, anomalous because it is capable of human speech. The girl, who always does as she is told, must wash the entrails of her friend, who has been killed because of its kind acts toward her. It is at this point in the flow of the story that the girl's fortunes are at their lowest ebb. This is a pivotal moment as well, since the girl's situation will now improve and the mistress' fortunes decline. Something valuable (gold) falls out of the offal; good comes from misfortune.

Cinderella, *on her own*, does a good deed. She creates order out of disorder and is rewarded by the fairies. This is the only positive act she commits in the story. Everything else she does, she does on instruction from others. She is the completely obedient child, and even here, in cleaning the house, she does voluntarily what she has been forced to do at home. When she returns with her gifts, she lies to her stepmother, but the lie is a virtuous act since she merely follows the instructions of the fairies. Her stepsister (who is also her opposite) goes into the tank. Although she obeys instructions and is, therefore, as dutiful as Cinderella, her acts, which create disorder out of order, lead to her downfall.

The common feature between Cinderella and her stepsister is the fact that both are obedient. In all other ways they contrast. The mistress and her daughter take an active role, while Cinderella remains passive. Although she does go to the races, she merely stands near the royal box; she *loses* her slipper accidentally, and when the King calls for women to try on the slipper, the mother and daughter go to the palace to try it on while Cinderella waits at home to be called. The story, which began with a senior woman seeking a senior man in marriage, ends with a man seeking a junior woman in marriage. In the first instance, the man resists actively while in the second the woman accepts passively. In the first instance, a pair of resistant boots which should prevent the marriage are destroyed (lost), therefore allowing the marriage; in the resolution, a pair of fragile shoes are not lost and become the means for consummating a marriage. Thus the story closes in on itself. Clearly the Cinderella tale is about kinship, conflict between generations, and step versus blood relationships. Cinderella's main virtue in this version is her obedience, but her stepsister is also obedient. What is more important is that obedience implies passivity as well. The mistress is active and aggressively seeks union with Cinderella's father and later with the King. This is clearly not the sort of feminine behavior that is rewarded in this particular tale. The mistress and her blood kin are finally punished for the actions of the mistress.

The immediate effects of Cinderella's obedient behavior are negative; they lead to the death of the cow. And in following the advice of her future stepmother in the first place, she had deceived her father; this deception is also the only selfish act committed by Cinderella in the story and she is punished for it. Later Cinderella emerges as the perfect housekeeper. She symbolizes correct feminine behavior and stands in contrast to the stepmother and her daughter who symbolize extreme unfeminine behavior.

The Cinderella story is widespread in Europe and versions can even be found in Africa and Asia. If individual units in these tales are changed, the basic structure will remain unaltered. I have seen versions from China and Africa, which vary, as might be expected, from the European version recounted here. The reader will remember that the mediator in the European version is a talking cow which, when killed, has its soft parts (intestines) put into water. In the Chinese version, the mediator is a goldfish living in the water. When it is killed, its bones (hard parts) are buried on the land. Thus the transformation of land animal for water animal is followed by the transformation of hard parts buried on the land for soft parts put into water. In this way, the over-all structure based on contrasts is preserved. In the African version, the mediator is, strictly speaking, neither a land nor a water animal, but a frog, an amphibian that lives on both land and in the water. In contrast to the other versions of this tale, the frog in the African version remains alive. In terms of structure, the mediator in the African Cinderella lies halfway between the European and Chinese versions.

Complex oppositions, inversions, and contrasts in narratives have the same effect as formal designs in visual art. They please the hearer or reader and provide aesthetic information in the context of structure. Bundles of significant signs are grouped into an emotion-arousing framework.

In the two examples presented above, apparently simple stories hide rather complex structures. It is these structures that provide interest and surprise. This is true despite the rather poor prose style in these particular renditions. Better style— richness of expression, good use of metaphor, attention to such factors as sound, irony, and variation in sentence structure— serves to heighten the aesthetic effect in well-written literature. Style enhances aesthetic power. It does this by interacting with the structure of a work. Style lies on the surface while structure is more or less deeply buried, depending on its complexity and subtlety. When the two interact, the aesthetic impact is immeasurably enriched.

Structural analysis allows us to uncover the underlying organization of a literary work (including drama and film). It reveals the organization of semantic information, the way in which it is formed into an aesthetic structure. It also allows us to see what kinds of symbolic systems are held in common in different works of art and even across different cultural traditions. Finally, it helps us to understand how a piece of literature works and can, therefore, deepen our appreciation of it.

Structural anthropologists divide texts into syntagm and paradigm. The syntagm of a text is its temporal flow as it unfolds from beginning to end. A paradigmatic analysis breaks the text up into bundles of related actions. It is in the paradigms that the meaning of key symbols and the whole emerges.

In the Cinderella story, the positive actions of Cinderella make up one paradigm and the negative actions of the mother constitute another. Frequently, different individuals in a story perform similar actions with positive or negative results. These actions may be grouped into paradigms. Paradigms reveal bundles of information that are arranged in formal patterns that produce an aesthetic response in the reader or spectator. A paradigmatic analysis of a text uncovers hidden meaning and at the same time shows how such meaning is converted into aesthetic structure.

The paradigm presented in Chapter 1 comparing Baruya initiation rites with scarecrow construction revealed an over-all structure that linked two cultural events into a coherent whole. That paradigm uncovered a set of covert symbolic relationships embedded in events that on the surface appeared to be unrelated. Such an analysis shows that symbols draw their full meaning from complex relationships that reverberate through a culture's symbolic domains. Taken alone, scarecrow making is neither ritual nor theater. Seen against initiation rites, its theatrical-ritual function becomes clear.

A structural approach to cultural material assumes that surface realities are only the outward manifestation of a hidden system of uniformities. Lévi-Strauss notes metaphorically, for example, that an examination of clock and watch faces from all over the world will never allow one to understand how these instruments work. Such variables as size, type of number used, shape of hands will have no significant relationship to the actual working of clock mechanisms. To understand how clocks work we have to look under the face to get at the machinery responsible for the orderly movement of minute and hour hands around the face.

Human culture cannot be understood only through the collection of facts about daily life. Such activities merely constitute the face of the machine. But unlike clocks, we cannot take human cultures apart to see what structures drive them. Instead, we must construct models in our heads that we hope are fair representations of the structures that drive the real behavioral system. These models will consist of elementary units and sets of relationships among them. The units themselves may vary widely, but it is the relationships among them that constitute a structure. These systems are said to have structure (the term "structure" can be substituted for "system"), in that a change in one relationship between elements will lead to a concomitant change in relationship among other elements. Yet the elements themselves can be changed without changing the over-all structure that is characterized by its sets of relationships.

In *The Savage Mind*, Lévi-Strauss illustrates his method by analyzing the system French people use in naming four categories of animals: pet birds and dogs, domestic cows, and race horses. He begins with the ethnographic fact that pet birds (in France, at least) are given human Christian names in accordance with the species to which they belong. This is followed by the hypothesis that birds are permitted to resemble humans not only because they are so different (this avoids conceptual confusion) but also because they share certain distinctive features with humans (they love freedom, live together in "houses," engage in social relations, etc.). Birds, then, are metaphorical human beings and, in addition, Lévi-Strauss notes, they are given metonymical names (names that represent part of a larger set, in this case the set-names for humans), i.e., Pierrot, Margot, Jacquot.

Up to this point the analysis might seem a bit farfetched, even trivial, if interesting, but Lévi-Strauss goes on to examine the naming of dogs and their place in French culture in the same way. Unlike birds, dogs live among men as part of the social order. But because they occupy a low place in this order, the French do not name them in the same way as they name humans. Instead they use a special series of names (Azor, Medor, Sultan, etc.), which are, says Lévi-Strauss, like stage names. These form a series that is parallel to the names of ordinary people. Dogs are, therefore, by virtue of their relationship to human beings, metonymical human beings with metaphorical human names. The double reversal immediately makes the data and the hypothesis more interesting, for Lévi-Strauss has begun to show an inherent order in the naming system. If one side of his equation is metaphorical, the other must be metonymical. A reversal of one brings about a reversal of the other; the system is maintained. The case is strengthened by analyzing the system of names applied by the French to cows and race horses. The final result is a paradigm that reveals a structure and its transformations.

The entire system reflects an aspect of French culture: the classification of domestic animals. It also reveals certain relationships between humans and animals that exist, at least unconsciously, in the minds of many French people.

A structural analysis is a means for decoding basic cultural statements about the world. It gets at the root of culture as communication and tells us how it is structured in the mind. Structural anthropologists do not claim that specific information is genetically coded in the brain, but rather that certain patterns of thought (kinds of relationships) are genetic in origin.

If thought is organized into structures, so are various parts of culture. For although culture is played out, at least in part, in real behavior it is based on the peculiar operations of the mind. The relationships between various cultural domains can be analyzed from a structuralist point of view. If we focus specifically on art and its place in culture, we find that it lies halfway between scientific knowledge and mythical thought. The artist, like a craftsman, constructs a material object, but this product is also an object of knowledge. It is both an analytical statement about the properties of the object and an anecdotal representation of it. The genius of the artist, writes Lévi-Strauss in *The Savage Mind*, comes from his or her ability to unite internal and external knowledge

> a "being" and a "becoming" in producing with his brush an object which does not exist as such and which he is nevertheless able to create on his canvas. This is a nicely balanced synthesis of one or more artificial and natural structures and one or more natural and social events. The aesthetic emotion is the result of this union between the structural order and the order of events, which is brought about within a thing created by man and so also in effect by the observer who discovers the possibility of such a union through the work of art (p. 25).

In "primitive" societies there is a strong relationship between art and sign systems. Art functions as a communication device known and shared by the entire group. (Most primitive art is religious and each object has a known, fixed meaning.) But in all societies, even those in which art is strongly iconic, art is more than just an imitation of the object. If art were only a representation it would tend to lose its function as a sign. In order to remain art, art must be situated halfway between object and language. It must represent the object, but have its own identity as a sign. This, however, applies best to visual art. Poetry uses language as its tool. The poet stands in the same relation to language as the painter stands to his object. Poetry itself exists between two conflicting operations: the integration of language and semantic disintegration. Poetry is at the same time a concentration and tightening of language and a disintegration and/or restructuring of ordinary meaning. Sign referents are contracted and expanded to meet the needs of poetic imagery.

While art began as sign, the evolution of writing as a more direct representation of language pushed artistic production toward the figurative. Writing taught us that signs could be used to apprehend as well as signify the external world; in Lévi-Strauss's own words, "to gain possession of it." As art became more figurative, as individualization was introduced into it, its semantic function began to disappear. The artist tried to imitate his model rather than signify it. The opposite of this process is abstraction, in which a signifier is maintained but the signified is lost. An evolution of art is implied in this discussion, for art moves from signifying to figurative to abstract. One could argue that art as representation proceeded its sign function, although I accept that the notion "abstract art" (at least, as art) is a late development in the evolution of the creative process. The reasoning behind this notion, however, is marred by an obvious prejudice against nonrepresentation art.[1]

[1] In a footnote on pp. 29–30 of *The Savage Mind*, Lévi-Strauss reveals his conservative bias against modern art: "Pursuing this analysis, one might define non-representational painting by two features. One, which it has in common with 'easel' painting, consists in a total rejection of the contingency of purpose: the picture is not made for a particular use. The other feature . . . is a methodological exploitation of the contingency of execu-

Lévi-Strauss compares realistic art to Impressionism, Cubism, and primitive art. The Impressionists, he says, tried to *represent* in a new way through the analysis of light and color. The Cubists, on the other hand, tried to restore the sign function of art. Through semiabstraction they went beyond the object to a more general level of signification. Cubism is different from primitive art, however, because it is unable to re-create the collective understanding of art that must lie at the base of its sign function. Cubism is art for the initiate only. Because the conditions of artistic production remain individualistic, there is no possibility for language to be established. Language is a group phenomenon, Lévi-Strauss says.

Modern art is a kind of anarchy. Primitive artists reject new forms since they are anxious to protect their own language, while modern artists constantly seek new styles, which results in a kind of "gratuitous playing about with artistic language." When we find nonfigurative art in primitive societies, it is either because it functions as sign or because there is a superabundance of the object that is portrayed. By this Lévi-Strauss means that the world inhabited by primitives is bound up with the supernatural in such a way that everyday experience is constantly in touch with extraordinary powers. When the artist attempts to represent this world, he cannot do so in a realistic way because the supernatural is by definition nonrepresentable. No realistic model of it can be made.

---

tion, which is claimed to afford the external pretext or occasion of the picture. Non-representational painting adopts 'styles' as 'subjects.' It claims to give a concrete representation of the formal conditions of all painting. Paradoxically the result is that non-representational painting does not, as it thinks, create works which are as real as, if not more real than, the objects of the physical world, but rather realistic imitations of non-existent models. It is a school of academic painting in which each artist strives to represent the manner in which he would execute his pictures if by chance he were to paint any."

On the other hand, as Lévi-Strauss is quoted by Georges Charbonnier in *Conversations with Claude Lévi-Strauss:*

> . . . abstract painting may present a system of signs, a system which has an intentionally arbitrary relationship with the object. But is the language which is imposed upon us willy-nilly a language which is still in contact with the aesthetic emotion, or is it not rather a system of signs like any other . . . ?
>
> The great danger threatening art seems to me to be two-fold. First, instead of being a language, it may become a pseudo-language, a caricature of language, a sham, a kind of childish game on the theme of language, which does not succeed in achieving signification.

In short, for Lévi-Strauss abstract art lacks the essential essence of art, which lies in its ability to offer a "kind of reality of a semantic nature." He is apparently so disturbed by this tendency in Western art that he ventures to say that after abstract art there may be no painting. On the other hand, he suggests there might be a counterreaction in the art world with a return to representation. He even goes so far as to predict the development of hyperrealism:

> Art may disappear or . . . are we not about to witness a complete reversal of this trend, a return to professional painting, to trompe-l'oeil . . . the re-creation of an objective world . . . ?

It should be no surprise that I have difficulty accepting the limitations that Lévi-Strauss puts on art. I think his error, beyond his inherent conservatism, is to fall into the trap of confusing art with language or at least failing to realize that the family relationships between the arts and between the arts and language, the essence of which *is* sign, does not imply a fixed set of game rules in which the sign must be embedded in the artistic product itself. The game, for me, is wider than this. It may lie in the idea surrounding the art, that is, the idea may be part of the art object even if it has no physical essence. The notion that Lévi-Strauss has (which is shared by many critics and laymen)—that craftsmanship is the common denominator of all aesthetic manifestations—is, I think, wrong, unless the notion of craftsmanship is extended to include the game itself. The Austrian philosopher Ludwig Wittgenstein once said: "Do not say he is playing the game badly, but rather find out what game he is playing well." A "badly" executed piece of art may or may not be bad art. If the game rules include "bad" execution and if the game itself is interesting, the art product may be interesting as well. It might even be good art! If an artist displays a plank of wood by leaning it against the wall of a museum, the form lies not in the plank, but in the game. Context changes the relationship between signifier and signified. Might we not add that this relationship is also changed by the rules of the game and the historical context in which the game is played? In a gross sense, art is a statement about humankind in relation to the natural order, a reflection of the basic dichotomy between nature and culture. On the level of social organization, it is a profound reflection, as is myth, of the inner conflicts and contradictions of the social order.

There is an essential difference between primitive and Western art. This difference lies not only in the close relationship between primitive art and communication, but also in the ties that exist between art and other aspects of culture. Primitive art reverberates within and across several symbolic domains, while modern art reverberates primarily within the domain of art and art criticism. While modern art may and probably does have profound psychological effects on those who respond to it, its major impact is on that small part of society that is the art world itself. Art in primitive society is an aspect of primitive culture, in all its richness and complexity. If modern art has a nonlinguistic cognitive function, which I think it does, this function must be much further removed from language than is the art of primitive peoples. The game of modern art is an *art game*, while the game of primitive art is in a much fuller sense a *cultural game*.

This does not mean that market forces and commercial activities play no role in artistic production in the West. Nor does it mean that art in non-Western societies has no function other than those discussed here. Art can be used in a number of ways, to differentiate social groups, to hoard wealth, to mark the boundaries of an ethnic group, to reinforce religious beliefs, or to provide individual pleasure to artist and observer alike. Most of the functions listed are culture-dependent, however, and rest upon the ease with which art can be used to carry a sign load because of its ancient relationships to language and communication.

As a method, structuralism has worked better in the analysis of literary texts than it has in the analysis of visual art. There are two reasons for this. First of all, structuralism works best when the material analyzed has both a syntagmic structure (a temporal flow) and a paradigmatic structure. Visual art, of course, lacks the temporal element. Second, Lévi-Strauss has tended to scatter his remarks about visual art widely rather than apply his method rigorously to a specific corpus.[2] In the

---

[2] In his most recent work, on primitive masks, *La voie des masques* (Skira, 1975), Lévi-Strauss does attempt to relate art to a set of associated myths. The analysis is only partially successful, however, because it deals with only two mask styles in a vast and complex corpus of art found among the Indians of the northwest coast of Canada.

analysis of visual art, particularly from preliterate societies, the visual material must be seen as part of a complex sign system linked to myth and its associated ritual. One must have a good sample of both types of material in order to relate transformations in the visual portion of the corpus to transformations in the mythic portion.

When it comes to modern art our problems are compounded. The structuralist approach may not work for modern art because in our society, art as an aspect of cognition is, in most cases, separated from the rest of our social and symbolic life. Remnants of structure may continue to exist, but these might well be more amenable to psychoanalytic interpretation than to structural analysis. Modern art has not, as Lévi-Strauss believes, lost its significance, but it has been cut away from the kind of coherent code system we find in preliterate societies.

The structural analysis of visual art must be concerned with both the physical context in which the art occurs and its mythic and social context. In order to give the reader some notion of what I mean by this, let me present a very simple, if incomplete, example. The analysis is drawn from the ethnographic work of Dennis Warren, who spent several years studying native medicine among the Bono people of Ghana.

The Bono, like the Abron among whom I worked, are an Akan people living near the border of the Ivory Coast in the west-central portion of Ghana. They are organized politically under a King and were incorporated many years ago into the Ashanti Empire. Many curing temples can be found in Bono territory. These are equipped with what are referred to as "brass pot" shrines. These shrines are literally sacred brass pots in which supernatural powers are thought to reside. In many of these temples, however, brass pots are found in association with a special group of sculpted figures. The shrines provide the physical context for these figures, and beliefs about sickness and curing provide the symbolic context. The figures are of three types: carvings of a nursing black woman with exaggerated breasts; bush devils (imaginary monster figures with a combination of human and animal characteristics); and white men dressed in bush jackets and pith helmets. The female figure, an African woman, contrasts with the white male figure in both color and sex. She contrasts with the bush devil because the latter is sexless and supernatural. On the symbolic level, she represents fertility and life while the bush devil represents disease, but only for those who transgress social rules. On a higher symbolic level, the context suggests that the female figure represents normal Bono culture while the white man represents alien culture, perhaps even superculture. The Bono are aware that European medicine is powerful and in many cases more effective than indigenous methods of treating certain diseases. Taken together, the two human figures contrast with the bush devil. The latter is an inhabitant of the untamed (and hence natural) realm and is a supernatural being as well. Since females often symbolize the natural order rather than the culture, the presence of the bush devil might operate as a marker for the female figure's cultural aspect. The brass pot is the only functional object present, yet is also the locus of curative power within the shrine. Although real, the brass pot is the only nonfigurative object present and may symbolize abstract power that is, according to African tradition, faceless, unknowable, and mysterious. As such, it dominates the other symbolic objects in the shrine, which although symbolic are also figurative.

These hypothetical relationships can be diagrammed as follows:

	BUSH DEVIL	FEMALE FIGURE	MALE FIGURE	BRASS POT
SEX	0	female	male	0
DOMAIN	nature	culture	superculture	super-nature
FUNCTION	−	−	−	+
OBJECT	symbolic	symbolic	symbolic	real
REPRESEN-TATION	figurative	figurative	figurative	nonfigurative
COLOR	black	black	white	metallic

The presence of a European male figure in the shrine fits Bono medical theory. Disease is often seen as the manifestation of social illness. When this is the case, both the proximate symptoms and the cause must be treated. Social illness can only be treated with Bono medicine. Many symptoms will respond to European treatment. The combination of these various figures in the Bono shrine, therefore, add up to a shorthand statement about Bono conceptions of disease and its cure. This is why the shrine with its full complement of symbols is ritually effective. Together, all the objects make up a culturally significant set that reflects both particular and universal aspects of structural organization. The oppositions present are familiar to us even if their context is not.

It may also be the case that this structure has aesthetic impact. Like most art, the shrine as a whole is an integrated set of concentrated symbols. It may, therefore, speak to individual Bono in both a ritual *and* an aesthetic language.

While I do not offer a fuller structural analysis (to do so would require more information than is available to me), I hope that this illustration indicates the direction in which such analyses of visual art must proceed. So far, no detailed work of this type has been attempted, at least in published form.[3]

Structuralism in anthropology as a theory and as a method offers many interesting insights into the relationship between art and communication and between communication and the social order. The method has been successfully applied to myth and, in some cases, to literature and films (see in particular the work of Peter Wollin). I have tried to show how the method can be extended to visual art, at least the art of non-Western peoples and even Western art up to the modern period. Structuralism provides a theory to account for the organization and integration into one system of semantic and aesthetic information. It helps us to understand why texts with the same semantic information may vary in terms of aesthetic value. Structural analysis also provides a means for decoding the semantic basis of visual symbolism, at least for those cultural traditions in which visual art is but one expression of myth and ritual.

Structuralists assume that the unconscious has a universal transcultural aspect. They also assume that the way in which the unconscious works in every culture can be revealed through the analysis of symbolic behavior. While structuralists realize that the content of any symbolic system is variable and determined by local cultural-historical factors, they assume that invariant relationships occur among the elements, or parts, of any specific system. If any element of a system is changed, other elements must change as well. Transformation, then, is only a means for the preservation of systems or structures.

[3] Two works that purport to be structural in nature (*African Art as Philosophy*, edited by Douglas Fraser, Interbook, 1974, and *The Structure of Art*, by Jack Burnham, Braziller, 1971) are superficial in concept and fail to employ the structural method as outlined by Lévi-Strauss and others.

The Artistic Animal

If structuralists are correct, the aesthetic response is a response to the arrangement of formal and symbolic elements in what has come to be known as art. This response reflects one basic aspect of human nature rather than the specific content of any one culture.

Chapter 6

"Good Form"

ALL ARTISTIC TRADITIONS have their conventions, which are either fully conscious or are so embedded in practice that they have become automatic aspects of artistic behavior, the way hair combing and tooth brushing have become automatic aspects of daily behavior for most Americans. We may not be aware of just how we perform habitual actions, but they do not follow the rules of the deep unconscious the way dreams do.

Successful art must meet the canons of "good form" (that which is universal in the aesthetic response), structure, and convention. Convention, or a set of normative rules, restrains to some degree the creative freedom of the individual artist. These rules are restricting. They provide the ground against which individual deviations are played. These deviations are not anarchistic, however. They must operate within a deeper set of rules based on form and structure. This might be clearer if we take an example from the realm of games. It is, for example, just as possible to be creative (to develop an individual style) in chess as in art, although chess has a set of rigid rules. Chess experts can usually identify a specific player by reading the recorded moves of a particular game.

Harold G. Schonberg, the music critic and a chess buff, wrote the following in his *Horizon* article "A Nice and Abstruse Game":

> A wrong move, a sloppy continuation, is as unpardonable and aesthetically shocking as a vulgar phrase in Mozart's "Dove sono" . . . for any artist can go mad with frustration when he finds that his conception is flawed—or, even worse, that he has ruined a brilliant conception by a stupid, obvious blunder. Artists hunt for the ideal; they spend their lives striving after a vision that no human can ever reach. No less than the other creative arts, is this true of chess, the youngest of them. . . . Whether romanticist or classicist, however, the great chess player is dealing with the elements of creation. Instead of notes on ruled paper, or oils, or stone, or words, he uses chess pieces. His aim is to take the raw materials and from them forge a continuity that expresses his own personality.

Art is not like chess in two important respects, however. An artist may create new rules as the limits of style are probed, whereas in chess the rules must remain intact. Convention in chess is the set of standard moves (the Queen's Pawn opening, for example) that have developed through time as style becomes *conventionalized*. Structure in chess is the set of rules that govern the game. It is frozen and conscious. In chess, both convention and structure lie on the surface, while in art, only convention is a surface phenomenon. In chess, both structure and convention are restricting, although the latter less so, while in art, structure is generating and productive. In art, structure provides an underlying order, but it is an order that transforms itself according to a set of internal unconscious rules. Thus in art, structure contrasts with convention. The artist may break the rules of convention but may never break the rules of structure.

The rules of structure are hereditary and coded in the brain. They transcend the barriers of culture. The contents of any particular structure, however, are strictly cultural. Structures are related to *how* we think, not *what* we think. Nonetheless, because structures deal with relations among elements, including the orderly transformation of these elements, they have a great deal to do with conceptual organization. This includes the organization of art. Artists are bound by convention *and* structure, but in different ways and in different degrees. They are often free—in fact, they are often required—to stretch conventional rules, but their final product must conform to a set of unconscious structural rules. What artists finally produce will also depend, of course, upon the school of art within which they operate, the materials they choose to exploit, the available tools and techniques, and the instrumental factor (use), if any, in the final synthesis, which is the finished art work.

The rules of structure and form (aesthetic universals) provide cognitive order, but this order is unconscious. The grammar of structure is not the grammar of ordinary discourse. Its possibilities are not the same as ordinary literal speech. Our ability to create metaphors, so essential to any art form, is due partially to this grammar, as well as to the relatively open nature of the symbolic process. If linguistic meaning were a closed system, if every term had a single unchanging set of referents, language would lose most of its flexibility, and its adaptive significance would be reduced.

When we employ or accept new metaphors or other kinds of

symbolism, we engage in transformation-representation. In fact, the tendency to manipulate symbols and impose sense on them is so strong in us that we are constantly receptive to new meanings. But to work as art, aesthetically successful metaphors must have something intrinsic in them as well. The intrinsic factor is based on form and structure.

Let me give an example of this, using the conventions of English grammar. When we read lines of computer poetry like those cited by Marie Borroff in her article "The Computer as Poet":

> *Let the tautology of your arm be reddened;*
> *Let the way of your hat be dissolved*

or

> *The roses are vomiting.*
> *Enough!*
> *How they squeeze their fierce ribs*

we strain to give them meaning because they are grammatical. When we see a line of poetry literally translated from a language distant grammatically from our own, we may not make sense out of it even if we know it is supposed to be poetry. But the relationship between "poetry" and everyday speech, particularly when grammatical sense is present, as it is in the case of computer poetry, at least, stimulates us to find the hidden sense that we are sure is present. Of course, knowing that the computer was "writing poetry" also helps us to impose meaning, for if the lines cited here were assumed to be prose we might well reject them out of hand.

If we manage to give meaning to these lines, we do so not only because they are set in a conscious grammatical frame, but also because they can be made to fit unconscious structures.

"Good Form"

The surface grammar which is a convention of language signals that sense *should* be present. When and if the sense is "found," it will have to conform to structural rules.

Each of the evolutionary processes discussed in this book has left its mark on the artistic process. Response to form appears to remain one fundamental characteristic of human behavior that persists, if only as a shadow, across the barriers of culture. The play element, coupled with exploratory behavior, reflects the noninstrumental aspect of art and, at least in Western culture, has become a conscious imperative of artistic production. We have seen how both the response to form and play-exploration in artistic behavior could be adaptive in nonartistic behavior. Transformation-representation linked to structure supports art as a cognitive process and in so doing, merges semantic and aesthetic information within the confines of form and content. Form and content are inseparable because they can only be manifested together through structure. It is structure that gives form to content and content cannot exist except in the context of form.

Art as fully emergent cultural behavior consists of three elements: convention, structure, and form. Form and structure are precedent to convention and each in their own way influences it. Convention is a culturally controlled set of styles and rules. Form in the rough, so to speak, is the physical manifestation of those patterns that trigger the aesthetic response. Structure, as we have seen, consists of relationships between elements of cognitive activity. It is subject to transformation according to a set of orderly rules. Structure provides art with its aesthetic information, the essential element in the noncognitive aspect of the aesthetic response. Structure is the way in which elements in an artistic product are arranged on the unconscious level. When children listen to the Cinderella tale, they are not consciously aware of the paradigms present, but it is these paradigms that contribute to the aesthetic impact of the story, that give it an over-all effect. Thus structure converts semantic information into aesthetic information. It is also, as has already been suggested, the link between the arts, at least in non-Western societies, as well as between the arts and other aspects of cognitive culture.

Because structure controls the way in which semantic information is organized into aesthetic information, it has both cognitive and emotional impact. Emotionally, it organizes information in ways that are aesthetically interesting (i.e., providing aesthetic information); cognitively, it plays upon the emotional impact of art to communicate with us with an immediacy rare in ordinary discourse.

Structure influences convention and is influenced by it. Both style and content are cultural elements in artistic production, but the juxtaposition of parts and the over-all form of a work of art will be partially dependent upon unconscious structure. Structure manipulates conventional elements according to its own set of rules. As the critic Morse Peckham says, artists must break conventional rules. I would add, however, that they are locked into a set of structural rules that determine how their choice of elements or units will be combined in the final product.

The stretching of convention does not break the bounds of structure. The same structure may be manifested in changed conventions. Convention is the familiar in art. Structure provides the aesthetic density in a work.

Let us see how these ideas work by posing a series of questions and attempting to answer them with the principles derived so far.

Why does some but not all nonsemantic disorder produce

aesthetic pleasure? We can turn this question around and ask why does some nonsemantic disorder produce displeasure? There are two answers. First, to produce pleasure, disorder must be patterned against order; against convention. This is Morse Peckham's answer and it is correct as far as it goes. Second, in successful works of art, form and structure underlie the apparent disorder. Therefore the surface disorder we can sometimes document in art is aesthetic because it conforms to rule sets that are as yet poorly understood.

Why does religious art maintain its aesthetic value (aesthetic density) for so long? Could it not be that it remains captivating by virtue of its secondary symbolic meaning that reaches us as a series of linked associations reinforced by structure? The awe produced by religion appears to be isomorphic with aesthetic awe or pleasure. As many philosophers have noted, aesthetic pleasure can be more than a simple enjoyment. It can be awesome!

How does an African mask work aesthetically for a non-African? It is a form. It is also (for a time) an aesthetic novelty. But sometimes this novelty persists, or, if it is not the novelty that persists, the appreciation persists. How much of the appreciation of works out of their cultural context is merely a response to "good form"? I suspect that much of the appreciation is linked to "good form" but that there must be structural elements as well that reverberate within those of us who respond. But then, where do these structural elements come from? Why was Picasso turned on by Dan masks from West Africa in the Musée de l'Homme? After all, visual art loses much of its semantic information when it crosses the barrier of culture. But the Dan mask also represents a face, a face transformed in a new way. Its impact lies in a new semantic message (expression) packaged in an aesthetic form. I don't wish to minimize the problem that exists here. As long as art is part of a cultural tradition, we can think of visual material as having structure by virtue of its relationships to other symbolic realms. The Dan mask in the context of Dan culture is tied to a particular ritual and its meaning is derived in part *from* that ritual just as it *provides* meaning *to* that ritual. The borrowing of art styles occurs frequently in Africa and other non-Western areas, but when it occurs, visual art is taken along with its concomitant myths and is incorporated slowly into the prevailing belief system. The Western art public is also capable of accepting art objects from other cultures, but it does so without the incorporation of associated symbols. In fact, these objects can be so easily accepted precisely because modern art has been cut away from a culture-wide code system. But if modern art and African masks in Western museums lacked all signification, they would also be totally devoid of structure. Our appreciation would fall back exclusively on our response to form. This cannot be the case, however, because one of the family resemblances shared by all the arts is that they incite subconscious symbolic activity. Modern Western visual art has not lost this characteristic. Our art is only partially cut off from structure. It is true that we have lost the connections between art and other symbolic domains, and this is a partial impoverishment, but we have also gained the ability to incorporate the art of other cultures easily into our own artistic universe. We have liberated the creative spirit from the cultural restraints that go along with ritual and mythic art. Modern Western culture is hungry for new art. This particular characteristic allows us to assimilate objects into those elements of structure that remain buried in the subconscious.

Is it presumptuous to say or think that art has always produced a "feeling" (subjectively) in the viewer? Is this empathy

13. Ceramic figure (6 inches high) from Nayarit, in western Mexico. The large head with flat face and the short body with stumpy limbs illustrate the conventions of a local style.

14. Ceramic pot (7 inches high), from the Recuay culture, central Peru, A.D. 200–800, a functional object transformed into art, is decorated with sculptures of a deity and attendants. Note the elaboration of the sculptures and the surface decoration on the body of the pot. The decorations are created by a process known as "negative resist." The artist covers the surface with wax, then engraves a design through the wax, and dips the pot in dye. The wax is then melted off, which leaves a negative design.

15. Hopi Indian dance wand (painted wood, 24 inches high), from Arizona. Completely flat, painted sculpture exemplifies one aspect of the Pueblo aesthetic convention, which contrasts markedly with African forms.

16. A great deal of natural talent is buried when children are taught the "correct" forms that art must take. These ceramic pots (7½ and 3½ inches high), by David Alland, fourteen years old, were made after three weeks of intensive study with an excellent potter who encouraged experimentation. The pots, which were fired in a wood kiln, display a certain amount of random, yet pleasing, decoration which results from the firing process. This is particularly the case with the larger one.

17. *Fun 1* (wood, cloth, plastic, and glass assemblage) by the American sculptor Jack Nelson. This version of Adam and Eve is a "pop art" representation of an ancient theme in Western art.

18. Two Karo Batak lizards from Sumatra, Indonesia. The one on the left, made of bronze, is realistic; the one on the right, painted on a house, is semiabstract. Both forms occur in different contexts.

19. A functional object from a European culture—an Art Nouveau inkwell (cast-iron, with painted surface, 8 by 7 inches) from France, c. 1910. Art Nouveau objects manufactured for daily use were highly decorated and sculptural in form.

20. This 1973 ink drawing (9 by 12 inches) by Julie Alland, twelve and a half years old, shows skill in design. Successful copying and imaginative composition are separate aspects of art. Many children are talented in one but not both of these areas, yet schools often reward only successful copying from nature.

we have with other supposed appreciators of art in other times and other places limited by our own cultural experience? But if this was the case, how could cross-cultural judgments of form ever be made? The Freudians are right: art is the language of the subconscious. Decoding begins with our response to good form. The presentational aspect of artistic symbolism binds our attention and liberates the subconscious. If this is true, then culture falls away. Real empathy across the barriers of culture means that there are panhuman mental patterns.

The real problem here lies in the question of whether structure can be inherent in visual art. If it is completely extrinsic to art, something that is tied to it culturally, then when an object is removed from its culture of origin, it must be automatically deprived of its structure. It is visual art that causes most of our difficulties. As far as verbal art is concerned, if structural rules are indeed universal and if structures are embedded in paradigms that unite semantic and aesthetic information, then exotic myths will produce an aesthetic impact. This will be true even if that impact is somewhat less strong among us than among members of the culture of origin. Our response will be weaker because we are members of a secular culture. Yet myths do retain a strong fascination for us. We are intrigued by stories about such mythical creatures as vampires and wolfmen even though they are, in the rational sense, totally rejected by our culture.

A different problem arises with music. Music is highly abstract, yet it is highly structured. Musical communication is a real phenomenon, but it is probably much further removed from language than is visual art. Because music has obvious grammatical structure, we might intuitively attribute a language function to it that it does not have. I do believe, however, that musical form exists in the same sense that good form exists in all the arts. Music arrests attention the same way that any other art form does. Our brains are keyed to respond to musical patterns in a way that is analogous to the way they respond to visual patterns. Music is communication, but not language.

Returning to visual art, we should recall that visual patterns are more than just form for humans. We are attributers by nature. Attributions are made both unconsciously and consciously. Just as we give meaning to a computer poem, we give meaning to an abstract painting. That is, we will give it meaning if we let it bind our attention, rather than reject it before it has a chance to work its magic on us.

When an artist says, "*I am trying to express myself,*" and when another says "*I am trying to express a universal feeling of X,*" and when another says, "*I am trying to express the form or essence of X,*" need we assume that they are saying different things? And if we believe that these artists are telling the truth, need we believe that they are correct in their judgments?

The expression of self in art must concern aesthetic form through which unconscious elements are aroused in the viewer. We empathize with artists in these cases, even if their message and our reading of it are totally different. Message and reading may be different because art once produced can be easily cut away from the artist. The artist loses control over the meaning of the work. Certainly, that part of the meaning that is cultural (by convention and partially by structure) is subject to change, but a residue of the original aesthetic information as contained in the form and the rest of the structure probably remains. This is the unconscious element.

Are there a limited number of good forms? "Good form" or "aesthetic form" is no more finite than language is finite. Language does, however, have a set of finite rules. Any formal system including both convention and structure must also have a set of finite rules. Although such systems have rules, these rules can generate infinite numbers of combinations. However, there should be forms that are not aesthetic and therefore cannot be included in the domain of good form, and there can be ill-formed structures as well.

What of the possible limits of art? Anthropologists have always had difficulty separating art from other human-made objects. The generally accepted dividing line is drawn between objects that have some intrinsic use and those which have no intrinsic use. The latter are included in the category of art. Unfortunately, no such neat boxes exist. Many objects of certain practical value appear to be decorated or worked beyond necessity. Are they to be included in the domain of art or not?

Humanity's first evidence of human environmental manipulation is stone tools. These are complex objects (simple though the first tools appear) that took a considerable amount of thought for successful manufacture. Are these stone tools art? By the middle Paleolithic period (at least 500,000 years ago) stone tools were refined in many cases beyond obvious utilitarian necessity. Does this refining represent a mere playing with form or is there some kind of transformation-representation present as well?

If a stick serves a child as a hobbyhorse,[1] is the stick art, for surely the stick-as-hobbyhorse is transformation-representation? The stick alone is not a playing-with form, for as object, the stick is not transformed. But the game rules in this instance do transform the stick, even if the child does not. The game in this case, however, is probably not aesthetic, although it certainly does involve transformation-representation. The making

---

[1] I borrow my hobbyhorse from Ernst Gombrich, *Meditations on a Hobby Horse and Other Essays on the Theory of Art.*

of the object (the mere taking of the stick by the child) is not playing with form *with the end of playing with form*. The stick is, rather, transformed instrumentally as the child plays with it. Playing horse is a fantasy game, but it is not necessarily an aesthetic game. Once the stick is decorated or made more horse-like, or both, is it then art or just more realistic? I find it difficult to use intention here as a guide. We must remember, however, that when toys are put in art museums they fall into the category of "found objects," which are considered to be art. Leaving the question of decoration aside for the moment, we can say that it is placement in the museum that constitutes the transformation-representation. It is the family resemblance between toys as game object and art as game product that confuses us here. Games are art only when they are consciously used as "found objects," archeological or otherwise. Returning to stone tools, we can say that their *overworking* (being worked beyond necessity) is a playing with form, a kind of doodling, but it is not art. Higher cognitive functions go into tools as the *tool aspect* of manufacture.

In the late nineteenth century, anthropologists and art historians argued whether or not a sequence of universal evolutionary stages existed for the development of art. There were disagreements even among those who agreed that art has passed through orderly stages. Some held that abstract art preceded representational art, while others argued the reverse.

Franz Boas, the founder of American anthropology and the great debunker of social evolutionary theory attacked both schools. Boas surveyed a vast amount of art produced by ethnic groups in recent times from all over the world and found that in some cases, where some historical depth could be documented, abstract forms precede representational forms and in other cases, the reverse process appears to have occurred. Boas was dealing in all cases with already evolved art forms. He could not concern himself with the first art because no one knows what it was.

Once artistic activity has fully developed, abstract representational, and expressionistic forms will certainly vibrate back and forth with changes in style and the direction of nonartistic ideological elements of culture. There are also cases of representational and abstracted designs existing at the same time with the choice of style dependent upon function, the media used, or the contextual placement of the art object. I suspect, however, that the first art *qua* art as I have defined it was representational, or pretty close to representational. Formal play, which we can see in the laboratory and sometimes even in the wild behavior of primates, precedes the emergence of our species, but art is at least one step beyond formal play. This step is not a small one either. For it involves the emergence of transformation-representation. It probably first occurred when someone living in a cave noticed that certain forms in the stone had the approximate shape of some natural object, plant or animal. The ability to see natural forms in clouds, for example, is itself undoubtedly a higher function and does not exist in nonhuman primates. Such perceptions involve the suppression of noise in those aspects of the image that do not conform to the "picture," as well as the filling in of missing information. Image reading of this type is no simple feat. Once images on cave walls or animal shapes in irregular stones were recognized as such, the next step was probably to improve upon them through retouching, by knocking away a bit of the stone or finishing a line with a bit of charcoal. This again was no simple cognitive feat. The form itself had to be perceived as a transformed representation of the real object, and a physical act had to be added to the perception, that act that realized the full expression of the partial form. Once this had been accomplished, the next step in transformation-representation was probably less difficult. Instead of retouching or filling, the artist created his or her own form. Once realistic animals were produced they could be conceived of as standing in for *real* animals. They became the signs for real animals. After this, the signs themselves became less realistic in the direction of either abstraction or expressionism.

The development of visual art was probably accompanied by storytelling and possibly by ritual. Most art historians and anthropologists are convinced that the first cave art had a ritual function. Surely the emergence of animals from the walls of caves through a process of discovery and retouching must have been a mystical experience that *had* to be verbalized. The first images must have struck awe into viewer and creator alike, and it would not have been a difficult step to go from this initial awe to its embodiment in ritual. The relation between seeing and telling, which I suggest began with the discovery of art, continued as long as art was the physical embodiment of cultural symbolism. Thus the structural relationship between verbal and visual art is both deep and natural.

Once the sign function of art had been fully discovered, one would expect to find very little truly realistic art. Instead, in most cases, art will reflect different degrees of abstraction and expressionism at different times and places, each related to the particular function of art within its cultural context. In fact, realistic art is almost exclusively limited to certain periods of the Western artistic tradition. Realism has been rare because it deprives art of its sign function. When it does occur, it is often in such items of tomb figures. These function culturally not as transformation-representations of the individuals portrayed (although, of course, they are), but rather as substitutions for the real person or animal so that they can reappear unchanged in the afterlife. Portraits of the living fulfill a similar function. They are meant to capture the living at a particular point in their lives so as to preserve them, at least metaphorically, for all time.

There are technical reasons why art is never an exact copy of nature. In representing nature, if that is what we want to do, we are forced to innovate techniques that, at best, approximate the model. This approximation results in a transformation. Once when I was sketching in the South of France I had to figure out ways of representing a particular type of vegetation that filled the background of my visual field. Finally I hit upon a technique that worked, although it was in no way a realistic portrayal of what I was seeing. I had done what artists do. I had taken a problem and solved it through transformation.

There is one problem with my theory about the origin of art. Before realistic art appeared toward the end of the Upper Paleolithic, abstract designs were made on small pebbles. If they had a magical function, they must have also had a symbolic function. If this is the case, and we cannot be sure that it was, I still don't think that these objects can be considered art. They were rather like the hobbyhorse—play with form, but not art.

There is a distinction between art, even abstract art, and decoration. Decoration frequently involves a repetitious, often continuous, design. It requires formal rules for its execution, and its aesthetic success depends upon principles of organization and balance (good form). The decorator is certainly an artist in the sense that he or she must play with form both in terms of choosing motifs and colors and in solving problems of application to different types of surface. In addition, even fully repetitious geometric designs can be, and often are, metaphoric representations of real or imagined objects or beings. Therefore, what has come to be called "decoration," is in fact art. But it is rarely very interesting art because it usually follows rules in slavish fashion. When the rules of convention are not broken, the art is dull. Part of the emotional shock or pleasure we get from art is due to the particular vision of the artist translated into a visual or auditory form. Decoration rarely surprises us as much as it might please us. In fact, decoration may be used as the background for variation. Symmetry is actually rather uncommon in art. One does, however, find symmetrical designs, particularly in architectural decoration. These function as backgrounds for shifting patterns that become part of the visual field. The movement of individuals in and around buildings changes the aspect of space and perspective as they see it. People moving within buildings contribute to an over-all visual pattern that is constantly shifting. The setting in which a building is placed may affect its static quality and transform it into a dynamic entity. The sun moving across regular sculptural detail may act to break symmetrical patterns and to change the decoration temporally through the daily and seasonal cycles.

Much of Islamic architecture involves repetitive motifs which act as a background for Koranic texts. The writing contrasts with the regular background and provides the eye with an element of surprise. Thus, in this case, two mundane forms (background decoration and writing) combine to produce what must be regarded as imaginative form.

Abstract art as opposed to decoration involves a game which the artist plays with form and structure in order to make personal statements through or about art. "But," one might ask, "if abstract art is nonfigurative, in what sense can it be transformation?" Asked in this way, the question prematurely eliminates abstract art from discussion. But let me pose the question another way: does abstract art enter into transformation-representational activity? The answer to this question must be yes. The artist (abstract or not) is always expressing something in terms of something else, and this, of course, is the essence of transformation-representation. Furthermore, abstract art as art only became possible with the discovery of representational art, for it is representational art that opens up the possibility for all art.

Let me now return to form, structure, and convention. Form is the armature for both convention and structure. If a work lacks good form, the art game is badly played, but we must always exercise care to be sure that we know where the form is located. Form may not be in the physical technique involved in the production of an art work, but in its essence, in the idea behind the game.

Good art is a system with low noise. That is to say art is highly ordered by form and by structure. Noise consists of undifferentiated stimuli which interfere with the transmission of a message. Art as art is attention binding and stimulates the aesthetic emotion. It is, therefore, at least in this sense, a message. Yet an artist can take noise and transform it into art. Art made of noise (some of the music of John Cage, for example) is, once more, the type of game in which the form lies not so much in the physical essence of the art but rather in the game itself. One of Cage's musical pieces consists of several radios placed on the stage and manipulated on cue by "players." The music is made up of whatever happens to be on the radios that are turned up during the performance.

In our own culture, at the present time, the game element in art is, for many artists, the predominant element. This is so much the case that the game is frequently divorced from physical form. One need only to think about "happenings" and "minimal art" to see that this is the case. It is this divorce that has led so many conservatives in the art world to cry out against modern art. For them the game must always involve craftsmanship in the shaping of the physical presence of art as either object or performance. These individuals do not bother to see what game is really being played and whether or not it is being played well.

There are major differences between the verbal and visual arts. Verbal arts have a temporal and therefore syntagmatic structure, as well as a presentational or paradigmatic structure. Yet visual art is exclusively presentational; it is there all at once. Whatever temporal flow it might have is dependent upon its associated myths and rituals. In myth and oral literature the full range of structure emerges only with the analysis of variants. The over-all density of symbolism and the complex paradigmatic relations emerge only with the flow of myths through space and time.

These differences can be reduced if we realize that painting and sculpture do not stand alone but are embedded in a psychological and cultural matrix that projects them from an immediate and presentational aspect into a discursive relation with the mythic content of their culture. Primitive art in this respect is richer than Western art, but the discursive elements in modern Western painting and sculpture have not been totally obliterated by the emphasis on form and originality imposed on them by our culture.

Chapter 7
Art and Society

JEAN COLLET, the French cinematologist, reports that after the first presentation of Alain Resnais's *Hiroshima, Mon Amour* at the 1960 Cannes Film Festival one of France's leading critics exclaimed, "*Hiroshima,* c'est la merde." This was not the first time that a critic's judgment has gone astray nor will it be the last.

In the December 1974/January 1975 issue of *En Route,* the Air Canada magazine, the following advertisement warned prospective buyers of fakes:

ESKIMO SCULPTURE
Be sure it's the real thing.

There is an increasing number of mass-produced imitations of Eskimo sculpture being sold today—clever imitations of no lasting value, but which can easily be mistaken for authentic art.

To be sure, when you buy Eskimo sculpture, that you get the real thing, look for the igloo tag. It is attached to every authentic sculpture and is your only guarantee of authenticity.

This tag is ironic because it signals the fact that authenticity is external to the object itself. The prospective buyer of Eskimo sculpture is no longer expected to be able to tell a real from a fake piece by examining it. In a sense, he is no longer expected to be a buyer of art but has become, rather, a buyer of commodities.

These two examples appear to contradict one of the major arguments of this book—that there is a nonvariant genetic element in artistic production and appreciation. To be sure, cultural elements can obscure whatever hereditary elements exist as the basis of judgment, and the assumption that "good judgment" is a combination of genetic potential *and* training. Sensitivity to art is, like most biologically based characteristics, a combination of nature and nurture. Yet the negative response to Hiroshima came from a well-known critic schooled in the cinema. How could he be so wide of the mark? Since its release, *Hiroshima, Mon Amour* has become an accepted film classic; an example of innovative and aesthetically successful cinematography.

Artistic innovations have been greeted negatively by a wide coterie of establishment critics. The Impressionist painters and later the post-Impressionists were met by derision in the professional art world. Final acceptance came about through public education pushed along in many cases by a new group of critics whose own reputations rose on the tide of a changed aesthetic among lay people. It was these critics who helped the art public to see in a new way. More recently the art critic Harold Rosenberg and the painter and art historian Robert Motherwell were the literary *avant-garde* for the "action school" of painting that developed in New York City in the 1950s. Once the change in aesthetic had occurred, of course, the new art became an important commodity and aesthetic judgment was no longer necessary to accumulate an impressive sales record.

The fact that buyers of Eskimo art, the production of which has become a major industry of the Baffin Island Eskimos, are no longer able to judge authentic works on their own is the result of commercialization in which it is not the art that counts but its investment value. Eskimo art has been degraded at two ends of the artistic process. Too much of it is being produced too fast with an obvious decline in aesthetic value, and too much of it is being bought purely as banking ventures. Even the trained eye will have difficulty distinguishing an authentic from an inauthentic piece. It is for this reason that contemporary Eskimo sculptures must bear the label of authenticity. Otherwise, they are indistinguishable from fakes.

The market value of art has always had an effect on its flow among the public, and Establishment critics have always a vested interest in maintaining that flow, even when they did not gain financially from it. In the West it was small groups of artists themselves, working on the fringes of the art world, who were most receptive to new forms.

A conscious desire to innovate, however, has proved to be inadequate for the flowering of a new style that successfully touches the emotional chords that produce the aesthetic response. Thus there are artists and critics who push the new like a steel plow through established concepts of good art. Their vested interest is to explode old concepts and make a place for themselves among the art-buying public. We know that these individuals succeed for a time, but their glory is often ephemeral in the light of historical forces that eventually filter out works limited in aesthetic scope.

Finally there is the art that succeeds for a short time, fades into the past, and then, at some later date, is reborn. Revivals of little known artists is a favorite game within the small world of critics and scholars. Here again we must distinguish between an aesthetic that has, for cultural reasons, faded with signs of fatigue in the public (perhaps because it meshed too well or not well enough with accepted conventions) from the conscious attempt to *re-establish* little-known artists for the sake of *establishing* little-known critics. We must also remember that the game of criticism contains many subsets of critics ranging from the avatars of popular taste to the aesthetes who are well schooled in the conventions of art and sensitive to the force of underlying aesthetic structure. Finally, there are the academics, particularly at the beginning or end of their careers, who must seek a path through the unknown to establish themselves among the ranks of professionals. Unfortunately, taste and criticism are only partially linked and both are subject to cultural forces that lie outside aesthetics.

Art is completely embedded in culture and will reflect or be controlled by culture to a greater or lesser degree, depending upon the nature of the relationships between art and other cultural areas. In primitive society, art is a central locus of a widely shared cognitive structure. It is a material manifestation of the intangibles of prophecy and belief. In our Western society, art is strongly affected by those market forces that pervade every other aspect of our daily lives. It cannot be understood apart from these forces, even though the aesthetic aspect is never totally submerged. In primitive society the artistic emotion is manipulated for symbolic ends, while in Western society it is often manipulated for economic ends. In both types of society it may also function as a marker of status, rank, or some other form of social differentiation.

It is for these reasons that art, as a part of culture, can only be understood from the point of view *of* culture. If art has a strong biological base, that base is manifested only in the context of a particular history. Art does not stand alone as a biological process, because one of its most important aspects, transformation-representation, takes its content from the specific moment. Art and transformation-representation are only realizable historically. Otherwise they remain nascent possibilities: sets of relations between empty categories, grammars without either language or speech. Structure is never totally apparent on the surface of things, but it is never independent of that surface. Convention seeps downward toward structure through the imposition of conscious categories that are reformed, sometimes distorted, and connected in new ways in structure.

The cultural-historical aspects of art force a certain relativism upon us, for all schools of art, wherever they occur, must be treated as individual phenomena with their own past, present, and future. But if we are to understand art as a process, we must suspend this relativism in an attempt to probe for those common elements that emerge from our biological past and reflect the basic structure of mind. Relativism is out of place in our search for the underlying uniqueness of our species, since it is manifested in those aspects of behavior that we do not share with other species. We must probe the foundations of this strange given "psychic unity" to find out what it is that sets the stage for the emergence of human consciousness and culture. We must come to understand how psychic unity combines with history to produce culture and how individual minds grow in the context of particular sociohistoric conditions. This is a difficult task because it is impossible to separate completely the biological and cultural in ourselves. If you deprive a human being of society and culture you destroy that which is particularly human. Our true nature is based on the cultural manifestation of nascent possibilities and limitations. Cross-cultural studies of invariant phenomena will shed some light on what it is we have in common. The investigation of cultural acquisition in children from within the perspective of single societies, as well as across different societies, will also make it possible to sort out some of the basic processes that unite us as a species and, in addition, will clarify those aspects of artistic activity that are truly variable.

Art is a specific human phenomenon even though its roots lie in our evolutionary past. The appreciation of good form does not emerge full blown in human beings, but rather has biological antecedents in other mammalian species. Fine-grain perceptual discrimination and high memory storage are gradual developments in the phylogeny of mammals. They see their highest development in humans but develop rapidly in all mammals and particularly in primates. Play and exploratory behavior are ancient capacities of mammals, all of which are equipped by their intelligence to make use of information through such activity. The only specifically human capacities that emerge in art are for transformation-representation and structure; and these, of course, are not limited to art nor have they emerged as a product of natural selection because such selection has favored artistic expression. Rather, artistic expression flows from transformation-representation and structure. It is made fully possible by them.

Aestheticians have often raised the question, "Is the appreciation of a sunset and the appreciation of a painting of a sunset the same thing or is each response somehow different?" In my opinion, they are different but related phenomena. The appreciation of a sunset is the appreciation of form, while the appreciation of a painting of a sunset, or any painting for that matter, is based on the appreciation of form plus a response to transformation-representation. The act of representing a sunset is an artistic act. The response to this act is also an artistic act. Looking at the painting, we must respond to what it is and what it contains. It is a transformation-representation and it contains form and structure. It is not merely the representation of nature, because the artistic act involves choice and emphasis and depends upon certain accepted cultural conventions which allow the painter to signify. Sunsets are read and known by observers of nature. Paintings are signified by a set of conventions that vary through time and space. All normal humans will be able to tell a sunset whenever and wherever they see one, but the same individuals might not be able to read a painting of a sunset if he or she did not know the conventions of the art in question.

Curiously, however, we must not stop here and throw out the reverse notion that artistic representation might affect our appreciation of natural beauty. From a cultural standpoint, certain natural phenomena may have been appreciated only after they were *first* painted. In the medieval period in Europe, for example, people closed nature out of their lives. Villages and cities were surrounded by walls, and streets curved in and out among the houses so that even the sky was partially shut out. In contrast, if you look down a street in an American town or city, in most cases you will see sky directly in front at the end of the long straight row of buildings. In European cities the horizon line is often blocked by the street that curves away from the viewer. When nature was presented by artists during the medieval period and even later into the Renaissance, it was contained by culture. Used as a background for architectural paintings, carefully modulated trees and hills faded rapidly into a highly ordered background. Nature alone was never depicted. Paintings out of doors emphasized the human element both in subject matter and background. The latter was usually limited to carefully manicured gardens, orchards, or vines. Open country was frightening territory for medieval people. It was the land of wild beasts and vagabonds. Roving bands of robbers inhabited the forests and plains, ready to attack those who hurriedly moved through a territory. People traveled to get from one place to another, from end point to end point, not to enjoy the countryside. The appreciation of landscape, both in painting and in reality, came much later and even in the early eighteenth century travelers were terrified by such extravagant aspects of nature as tall wild mountains and rushing rivers. Such natural phenomena came to be the traveler's objective only after nature had been tamed by some artists who, in the Romantic period (mid-eighteenth to mid-nineteenth centuries), turned from domestic scenes to the more spectacular aspects of the natural world. In these cases it was the representation of nature on canvas that eventually led to a general appreciation of the real thing.

I have suggested that while it might be extremely difficult to say that something defined by someone as art was not art, judgments about good and bad art might be somewhat easier to make. This is because it is difficult to separate anything created by humans from the realm of art if someone (anyone) wants to place it there. The creative process is not limited to artistic production. Along with artists, good chess players, scientists, and mathematicians are creative. The word "aesthetic" has been applied to work when it is successful by the criteria of each profession, not by the criteria of art. There is no linguistic error in this. In fact, common usage of the terms "creative" and "aesthetic" point to the fact that the behaviors described fit into the same class, or at least into overlapping classes. All involve fine-grain perceptual discrimination; an appreciation of form (or, at least, formal rules); elements of play (even if the goals are not autotelic, the best work in science and mathematics is done in a protected environment in which "free play with ideas" is encouraged); and transformation-representation. These are the factors that gave rise to art, but are not exclusive to art. In addition, the products of these activities follow conventional rules, have structure, and appear to produce the same emotional response that is produced by form in art. It would be a mistake here, I think, to go so far as to say that chess games, mathematical proofs, and scientific discoveries have the same form or same "good form" as art. Form must also differ among music, painting, and the linguistic arts. Mathematical proofs and scientific discoveries do produce pleasure which may be dependent upon structure. Such mental operations are therefore difficult to separate from the aesthetic response. As is so often the case ordinary linguistic usage points the way to a real relationship. The best we can say is that the aesthetic response is a response to symbols and structure *as* symbol and structure. If they reflect ideology as they frequently do, they reflect it in a unique way. Art is an encapsulation of ideology in the physical presence of the art itself, whether this be a painting, a poem, or a symphony.

If we agree that it is difficult to talk about nonart in the realm of art, can we talk about "good" and "bad" art? Here the answer must be yes, but only tentatively so. We can begin with form. If there is such a thing as good form then there should be certain cross-cultural criteria that define it and allow us to predict with some success what art will be accepted and what art will be rejected (at least, the statistical frequency of acceptance or rejection). But these criteria apply *only* when form is located in the object or performance itself. This is not always the case, particularly in modern art. There has been an evolution of art from the original discovery of transformation-representation of natural forms to an extension of the game rules about form from objects to certain nonphysical or intellectual aspects of the game itself. When this happens, it is difficult to make decisions about good or bad art with the criteria of physical form alone. One has to know more about the game being played.

Convention is not a good guide either. In fact, it is probably the least valuable guide in judging art since conventions are strictly cultural and time- as well as space-dependent. If one cleaves too closely to convention as the basis of aesthetic judgment, one runs the risk of being left behind along with all those conservative critics who refuse to see the value in new movements. A good critic must always be wary of convention as a criterion for judging art.

Structure is another matter, however. A thorough analysis of structure can inform us as to the richness of novelty in an art form as well as to the density of its content. Eventually, structural analysis might be able to provide our judgments with some mathematical precision. It might tell us why perspicacious critics respond favorably to works that have yet to strike a chord in the general public. Such analysis digs into the content of semantic information and reveals its arrangement in structural patterns that may be the foundation of second-order form. It also allows us to see the ways in which a single work of art is covertly related to other works. Since such relationships may themselves contribute to the aesthetic impact of a work, any method that unlocks these difficult and covert relationships tells us something fundamental about art as product and activity.

Creative art is an extremely complex phenomenon. While structural analyses allow us to understand partially why and how a certain work of art succeeds, no one has been able to

reproduce or generate a work of art by using structural principles alone. Structuralism informs us about mythic structure,
but it does not generate myths. It informs us about literary
structure, but it does not generate literature. There are two
reasons for these limitations. The first has to do with the little-
understood role of good form in successful art. The second has
to do with the basic complexity and subtle flexibility of the
human mind. Human mental operations, particularly those
implicated in the process of transformation-representation and
other language functions, are qualitatively and quantitatively
more complex than those of even the most sophisticated computers. Models of mental operation based on computer simula-
tion fall wide of the mark. Studies of chimpanzee language acquisition fail for the same reason. Chimps can learn a great
deal in the laboratory. They are capable of rather spectacular
feats in the area of communication, but as yet they have not
learned language. And they do not produce art.

Current models of cognitive analysis are not capable of artic-
ulating form, convention, and structure together. Nor can they
deal with those ineffable qualities that go into the making of a
successful work of art. Good art shows the human hand. Good
creation is not the same thing as good dissection, and while
many critics have been able to decompose art, exposing its
strengths and weaknesses, few have been able to produce it.
When they do so, it is because they are artists and not because
they are critics.

In his article on chess cited earlier, Harold Schonberg tells us
that after ten moves the chess player is faced with a choice
of one move out of 165,518,829,100,544,000,000,000,000,000
moves. Most of these are wrong! If a player makes an error
at the tenth move in a master chess match, it can mean that he
is destined to lose. The artist, particularly in the verbal arts, is

faced with a similar range of choices when faced with the problem of expressing an idea. The probability of error might not be as large in art as in chess, but the probability of success in aesthetic terms must be quite low, for otherwise there would be many more successful artists. Schonberg notes that if a computer could work at the rate of one possible move per micromicrosecond, it would still take 10^{90} years to scan and choose the first move. This means, according to the author, that a computer would probably not reach the middle game in a thousand billion generations. In addition, while computers might make "perfect" moves, they cannot make unpredictable moves. There is some process in the human brain that is not yet understood that makes both good chess and good art possible. There is little doubt that it is related to language function and evolved as selection pressures favored the higher speech functions, which are controlled by both hemispheres. To believe that selection could have favored artistic production or complex game playing alone would lead to a parody of evolutionary theory.

In referring to art, critics have often used the terms "authentic" and "inauthentic." This is not quite the same thing as "good" and "bad." Generally, the term "inauthentic" is used to label an art form that either does not come from the people (at least, in primitive and peasant societies) or that is somehow imposed on a public through the manipulation of symbols arising outside of the artistic universe. If people are convinced, for example, that Eskimo art is socially or financially valuable, a wide public may come to collect it. Finally, it may be copied and its original forms distorted as it turns into a mass-produced commodity. What began as an "authentic" art may be transformed into "inauthentic" art.

The term "kitsch" has come to be associated with poor quality mass art in modern industrial society. The popularity of kitsch is said to rest on a debasement of taste in a society manipulated by the mass media. Mass art, instead of coming from the "people," is said to come from the manipulators of taste and is imposed on the masses by the media controllers. Those who do not like the programming most common on commercial television often refer to it as "kitsch." In this case, it is claimed that, for commercial reasons, the general run of TV programs is aimed at the large, middle class, buying public that has bloomed in advanced capitalist society.

Many years ago the anti-Establishment critic Dwight Macdonald, who is also a political radical, attacked both lower- and middle-class art in America in an article titled "Masscult and Midcult." The latter term was applied to the middle-class, book-buying public that favored well-written, competent, but not exciting art. Macdonald was attacked by many as an elitist. It is a curious fact that many critics of mass- or middle-class art are radicals who take elitist positions in their call for art that caters to a smaller public, produced by better but fewer artists. On the other side of the coin, we find totalitarian systems that favor mass art of a particular kind. In the first half of this century we saw the rise of "socialist realism" in the Soviet Union and of Nazi art in Germany.

A look at the anthropological record reveals some interesting facts about popular art among nonliterate and peasant peoples, particularly those who have had the least contact with advanced industrial society. In most cases, the art produced in these cultures is considered by Western critics to reflect high aesthetic value. Of course, one could argue that, as exotic material, it appeals to our cultural need for constant stimulation from new aesthetic forms. However, this is a gross oversimplification. Primitive art was first recognized as aesthetically valuable by artists who were themselves innovators in Western culture. But it did not have a wide appeal to the general public, and even today mass-produced "exotic" art finds more favor with the Western public at large than good quality native art. Sensitivity to new forms is not a general characteristic of the Western middle class even when it is pushed to consume more and more goods and symbols by the producing sector of society.

When these very primitives whose artists have created many fine examples of "authentic" art become even partially absorbed into the Western industrial world, their general taste rapidly reaches the lowest common denominator found in the West. This is the case with so-called airport art from Africa which can be found in many cheap stores in the West. This phenomenon is partially due to the undercutting in Africa of local religious and symbolic systems. Without these, native art loses a major aspect of its *raison d'être*. Art in these societies is not just secularized, however: it is destroyed. Is it strange to see authentic art linked to a traditional symbol system become poor art linked to commercialism in a consumer society? I think not, because if aesthetic production is embedded in some aspect of culture that lies outside the realm of art, it might flourish in one context and be totally or partially destroyed in another.

What happens to art in these primitive societies and our own is that its structure is distorted and transformed while its conventions are debased by mass production. Concern for good form disappears along with the transformation of structure into an industrial mode. It is not that industrial goods cannot be aesthetic, but rather that producing them takes a rarely made effort and requires money. High-quality, aesthetic industrial production requires managers to employ experts who add "unnecessary" expense to production—at least, as such things are figured in cost accounting. As far as profits are concerned, there will of course be none unless the public responds and higher sales result. But since public taste has already been debased, why bother to improve it? Or so goes the reasoning.

Today, mass art displays a certain naïveté in relation to elite art. This is due, no doubt, to the buying of skill and talent by members of the upper classes who consciously use elite art as one marker of their high status. The upper classes still use art this way but, in addition, they have unconsciously deprived the masses of access to skilled craftsmen, who have become a rare commodity in the industrialized world. Those who train to become artists often come from the intellectual elite. They are trained to produce for the financial elite. The masses are trained to be producers of consumer items and consumers of their own production. They have no inclination themselves to return to a craftsmanship stage, which requires long apprenticeship as well as financial hardship. Most workers in modern factories work for their wages only and take little pride in their production. Leisure time is spent primarily in nonproductive activity.

While machines can produce excellent quality goods that are well designed and aesthetically pleasing, the finer crafts and art itself must come from those who put their personal mark into the production process. Such goods are expensive and have only a limited market. The rise of handicrafts among many of our young who have rejected consumerism has led to the overproduction of such items as pottery, woven goods, well-tooled leather, and jewelry. Much of this production is aesthetically good, but few of the artisans involved in producing are able to support themselves.

In a class-based society, particularly one in which there are vast subcultural differences, it has been suggested that each distinct group has its own set of aesthetic values. These should not all be judged ethnocentrically according to the aesthetic standards of only one group. The most recent advocate of this school is the American sociologist Herbert J. Gans. In his book *Popular Culture and High Culture* he suggests that popular culture reflects the aesthetic of the majority and is, therefore, an aspect of culture rather than a commercial menace. He adds that all people have a right to the culture of their preference regardless of whether it is high class or popular. Gans believes that the distinction between high- and low-class culture is an oversimplification and that the assumed differences between these categories has been exaggerated. He would substitute a fivefold division into what he calls "taste cultures," each with its own art. These are said to differ mainly "in that they express different aesthetic standards." Gans goes on to say that

> Because taste cultures reflect the class and particularly educational attributes of their publics, low culture is as valid for poorly educated Americans as high culture is for well-educated ones even if the high cultures are, in the abstract, better or more comprehensive than the lower cultures.

Gans criticizes the concept of mass culture and attempts to refute a set of major themes emphasized by those who characterize mass culture negatively:

1. Popular culture is mass-produced for profit.
2. Popular culture borrows from high culture and debases it.
3. Popular culture produces spurious gratifications and is potentially harmful to its audience.
4. Popular culture reduces the over-all level of cultural quality and encourages totalitarianism by creating a passive audience.

In reference to the first theme, Gans says that the producers of both popular and high culture look for emotional rewards from their audience. The creators of popular culture fight for their ideas and self-expression as fiercely as the creators of high culture. Thus popular culture cannot be characterized as an art form produced purely for profit. The second notion—that popular culture borrows from and debases high culture—is refuted easily. Gans points out that each borrows from the other. Furthermore, even if borrowing should occur in one direction, from high to low, high culture could continue to exist on its own terms. Certainly, artistic innovation within a culture is often the result of the internal circulation of ideas, symbols, and styles among segments of the population.

Gans protests against those who characterize the effects of popular culture as brutalizing or who say that it reduces its audience to a narcotized state unable to cope with reality. These are extremist views and Gans refutes them easily. He notes that among the effects that the mass media *have* had on the public is an acceleration of the demise of folk culture. Popular culture is, he tells us, almost always more attractive to people than their own folk culture. Yet this begs the question of why such choices are made.

Gans sees no evidence that popular culture has lowered general standards of taste. He says that the apparent decline is the result of selective memory among the critics of popular culture:

> Writers such as Oswald Spengler and José Ortega y Gasset remember only history's Shakespeares and Beethovens and forget their less talented colleagues whose work has been lost or ignored. Similarly, they remember selected kinds of folk art, but forget others that were more brutal or vulgar than anything in today's popular culture.

He also accuses the critics of popular culture of selective memory when it comes to mass art and totalitarianism. While he admits that Nazi and Stalinist art reflected a particular kind of political system and operated to promote it, this has never been the case in England and the United States, two of many nations in which mass art exists. In addition, while he admits that popular culture can be used by the state to promote its ideas, he reminds us that ideas cannot by themselves contribute to the establishment of totalitarian systems.

In his over-all attack on the critique of popular culture, Gans suggests that high culture is creator-oriented while popular culture is user-oriented. From this flows the idea that culture either belongs to those who create it (elite art) or those who consume it. In the latter case, one can ask to what extent culture is meeting the needs of its public, certainly a question that reflects concern for the members of society at large. The reason high culture fears popular culture is that it needs an audience just as much as popular culture. It fears that its audience will be wooed away by a user-oriented culture. High culture, therefore, needs to attack popular culture, especially when the latter borrows from the former, for it converts its content into a user-oriented form. Finally, high culture must think of popular culture as of low quality in order to maintain its own values against the background of popular culture.

Gans believes strongly that all human beings have aesthetic urges. These are shaped and channeled by the values and standards of the society in which they occur. He argues therefore that if people seek aesthetic gratification and if "their cultural choices express their own values and taste standards, they are equally valid and desirable whether the culture is high or low" (p. 127). Thus it is wrong to compare taste cultures alone. Instead, one must compare the taste publics who choose them. Gans admits that high culture may in fact be better than low culture, but this does not give society the right to prevent individuals from having access, to the taste culture of their choice: "I do not believe that all taste cultures are of equal worth, but that they are of equal worth when considered in relation to their taste publics" (p. 128). Therefore Gans ends on a democratic note. Our society should promote maximized opportunities for education so that everyone can choose from the higher-taste cultures. Until this occurs, however, it is wrong to expect individuals in a society with a low mean education level to choose only from taste cultures requiring a college education. As long as this inequality continues, it is also wrong to expect members of the lower-taste culture to support high culture. It is also wrong to criticize people who hold aesthetic standards that reflect their educational background.

Gans has defended these views in the New York *Times* in February 1975. His conclusion in this article is that the popular arts should be subsidized. This position is opposed in a companion article by the Dutch-American sociologist Ernest Van Den Haag. Van Den Haag accuses Gans of trying to convince us that "bad things are as good as good things, since both satisfy tastes which differ only owing to basic differences in American society." This is, of course, a distortion of Gans's position, which is much more subtle and complicated than Van Den Haag would have us believe. The latter goes on to repeat the points Gans argues against in his book and reaffirms his own view that "Beauty is not in the eye . . . of the beholder . . . even though a trained mind is needed to perceive it."

As long as Gans is willing to concede that there may be, if only from the point of view of the producer, certain quasi-universal standards, I find little to quarrel with in his book. His arguments are aimed at the kind of elitism advocated by Van Den Haag, who ignores the role of social factors in the complicated world of art. I agree with Gans that not all "high culture art is of high aesthetic quality" and that there is much of value in art born in the lower classes or in different ethnic groups. Rock-and-roll music at its best is a valid art form. So is jazz. While both have roots in black culture, rock and roll is a blend of many cultural elements. Its emergence as an art form came about in 1962 when four young working-class Englishmen—the Beatles, from Liverpool—added their own creative energies to an established musical style. Unfortunately, however, rock and roll has decayed of late, and much recent work in this area is sterile and uncreative. Part of this decline is due to cultural fatigue. (The great days of the English madrigal did not last much longer than the best of rock music and it did not have to contend with the industrial era.) But it is also caused by the commercialization of this as well as other forms of popular music. The industrialization of the arts may not, as Gans says, inhibit all creativity, but it does have a negative effect on many young musicians. The fact that new writers have tremendous difficulty in getting their first work published is another indication of how the commercial world can block public access to talent. There is a constant and growing tendency in the art market to play it safe with established artists. It is perhaps easier to be a painter or sculptor in American society than any other type of artist because the galleries are always looking for new visions in the quest for innovation, which is most in demand at the present time in the visual arts. Nonetheless, as aspiring young artists know, it is hard to get a first showing in a well-known gallery.

The commercial world of mass art has not done all the damaging things it is accused of by writers such as Dwight Macdonald. But if industrialization has to any extent contributed to a muting of creativity and a leveling of culture, it is in damaging the aesthetic potential that is the heritage of all human beings. Popular culture wipes out folk culture, not by insidious means but because individuals exposed to popular culture tend to choose it over their own indigenous forms. This means a loss in variety and quality. Unfortunately, the reasons why popular culture is so readily received are probably not central to art but are linked to other cultural factors in the economic sphere.

When the dominant form in society shifts from a folk or kinship base or from deep religious roots, the society's art is rapidly stripped of its structural relations to those domains of culture that give it its vitality and meaning. After that, it is easy prey to commercialization.

The fact that most Americans, regardless of social status, are caught up in the debased art of a consumer society does not make this a good thing. Art is not determined by majority vote. The fact that mass art is often, if not always, a poor imitation of high culture or a poor imitation of its own potentialities is not good either. We must be tolerant of different tastes, for it is variety in taste that allows the arts to develop. While artistic production and appreciation may have a genetic base, taste is a much more complicated matter. An individual's response to art is conditioned by an experience with art and with life in general and by the particular state of a culture's symbolism.

Popular art should be subsidized, but the best solution to this problem might be to subsidize those art forms that have wide appeal across the barriers of culture and class. There are artistic productions that have been accepted on all levels of society. I suspect that the major difference between good mass art and the art of high culture comes from the complexity and esoteric nature of the intellectual content of a particular work. Art that has a wide appeal to a heterogeneous public is art that has good form and either simple structure or a structure that is open enough and so widely felt because it reflects shared symbols that multiple reactions are set in motion by its perception. There are art forms whose conventions are not class limited and which can be built upon good form and structure. Mythic films such as the original *Frankenstein* (1931) are works of art that have wide public appeal and which continue to live among cinemaphiles. The *commedia dell'arte* in its time had a similar appeal. James Joyce's *Finnegans Wake*, on the other hand, is not for everyone since it demands a certain kind of intense education and attention to art.

But *Finnegans Wake* is not a good example of art for everyone. As long as our society is divided and pluralistic, wide differences will exist in the degree of sophistication among individuals and groups. There will, however, always be art forms that can appeal to all social levels. These are certainly worthy of public support. But there is no reason to limit public support to this type of art. Experimental forms that have only a limited audience may provide the symbolic variety that breeds good art. Artistic experimentation is important because it is a major form of symbolic exploration. The richness of culture depends upon variety and this variety supplies us with the ability to adapt to a wide range of changing environments and social conditions.

Art has become a fully cultural behavior, but it has not lost its biological imperatives. It still encapsulates and realizes the subconscious symbolic order and provides innovative stimulation as well as cultural continuity. Among all the forms of play that exist in our species, artistic play is probably the most important for cultural exploration. When creativity in the arts is stifled, the human imagination is immediately impoverished and a distinctive adaptation threatened.

The paradox of Western culture is that while our art public is open to creativity to an unprecedented degree, the scope of that public has diminished. Art was always produced by specialists, but our society is the first in which the art public itself is also made up of specialists.

If the foregoing explanation works, it works best for those periods in human history and culture in which art was very much a feature of the social fabric, functioning as a central part of the symbolic order. The emergence of art in modern Western society as a relatively autonomous domain has created problems that have been solved only tentatively. In the art of preliterate societies, structure can be teased out of such cultural data as myth and ritual particularly when rich ethnographic material is available. If structure continues to play a major part in Western visual art, it will have to be teased out of common elements in the unconscious. This is a much more difficult and scientifically ambiguous task, for we must turn from culture to the individual psyche. As an anthropologist I am more comfortable with cultural than with psychoanalytic materials.

However, while there are universal aspects of the unconscious, they are mobilized in different ways and for different ends in primitive society and in our own. In primitive society where what Lévi-Strauss refers to as *pensée sauvage* (savage mind) prevails, the unconscious is tied directly to the coherent system of symbols that makes up the culture-wide cognitive system. In our society the unconscious operates with a certain degree of autonomy. It has become the domain of our interior lives. Because art is no longer the glue that binds the dominant aspects of our cognitive system together, it can function in a more personal and private way and reflect different taste cultures. Nonetheless, the unconscious is activated in all cultures, including our own, by art in its many forms. It is in the domain of art that unconscious symbols are realized and externalized.

While myth is now peripheral to our lives, we have not lost

our taste for it. The cinema is a perfect medium for the realization of myth and it is in the cinema that we find a strong residue of common symbols. Mythic films, particularly in the science fiction and horror genre, do not succeed for so many of us because their scripts are of high quality (they are generally as illogical as the myths of primitive peoples) but rather because they mobilize the unconscious by means of a dreamlike visual mode. They realize myth and the dream work at the same time and revive our own *pensée sauvage*.

This book is speculative. Topics such as art as unconscious communication and aesthetic universals still need to be explored. In the area of visual art we need to know how culturally mediated artistic behavior develops in children. This should reveal those aspects of the aesthetic that are universal and those that reflect specific cultural traditions. There are many studies of children's art from many cultures, but so far none of them has been undertaken with sufficient controls to make an objective comparative study possible. Therefore many of the questions raised in this book remain unanswered.

The anthropological study of the creative process has only recently begun. In the past, primitive art was studied primarily out of context in the museum. Few studies of artists in preliterate society were undertaken and generalities about art and art making were based on speculative judgments. This situation is now changing. We have already learned that notions about aesthetics exist in societies other than our own and that ritual, myth, and those objects that we would classify as visual art involve both religious and aesthetic inputs. Rituals are sacred events, but in most cases they are also enjoyed by participants who judge performance on the basis of aesthetic merit as well as religious efficacy. We have learned that individual artists leave a personal mark on their works and that past art historians have tended to exaggerate the static nature of what is still called "primitive art." We are now beginning to see that wherever the art game is played, it is played according to similar rules.

Bibliography

CHAPTER ONE

Osgood, C. *Ingalik Social Culture*, Yale University Publications in Anthropology, Vol. 19, No. 53. New Haven: Yale University Dept. of Anthropology, 1958. Pp. 119–21, 127.

Tomkins, C. Profile: Robert Rauschenberg, *The New Yorker*, February 29, 1964. P. 71.

CHAPTER TWO

Caillois, R. Riddles and images. *Yale French Studies*, Vol. 40, 1968: 148–58.

Gardner, H. *The Shattered Mind*. New York: Knopf, 1975.

Gombrich, E. H., and Q. Bell. Canons and values in the visual arts: a correspondence. *Critical Inquiry*, Vol. 2, spring 1976: 395–410.

Freud, S. The relation of the poet to day-dreaming. *Collected Papers*, ed. by E. Jones, Vol. 4. New York: Basic Books, 1959. Pp. 174, 182–83.

Moore, O. K., and A. R. Anderson. Autotelic folk models. Paper presented at the meeting of the American Sociological Association, New York, 1960.

Morris, D. *The Biology of Art*. New York: Knopf, 1962.

Rosengarten, T. *All God's Dangers: The Life of Nate Shaw.* New York: Knopf, 1974.

Schiller, P. Figural preferences in the drawings of a chimpanzee. *Journal of Comparative and Physiological Psychology,* Vol. 44, 1951: 101–11.

Smith, D. A. Systematic study of chimpanzee drawing. *Journal of Comparative and Physiological Psychology,* Vol. 82, 1973: 406–14.

CHAPTER THREE

Bernstein, L. *The Unanswered Question: Six Lectures at Harvard.* Cambridge, Mass.: Harvard University Press, 1976.

Child, I. Personality correlates of esthetic judgment in college students. *Journal of Personality,* Vol. 33, 1965: 466–511.

——. Esthetics. In G. Lindzey and E. Aronson, eds., *The Handbook of Social Psychology.* Vol. 1, 2d ed. Reading, Mass.: Addison-Wesley, 1968. Pp. 853–902.

——, and L. Siroto. Bakwele and American esthetic evaluations compared. *Ethnology,* Vol. 4, 1965: 349–69.

Ford, C. S., E. T. Prothro, and I. Child. Some transcultural comparisons of esthetic judgment. *Journal of Social Psychology,* Vol. 68, 1966: 19–26.

Gardner, H. *The Arts and Human Development: A Psychological Study of the Artistic Process.* New York: Wiley, Interscience Publications, 1973.

Iwao, S., and I. Child. Comparison of esthetic judgment by American experts and by Japanese potters. *Journal of Social Psychology,* Vol. 68, 1966: 27–33.

Koch, K. *Rose, Where Did You Get That Red? Teaching Great Poetry to Children.* New York: Vintage Books, 1974.

Kohts, N. Infant ape and human child. *Scientific Memoirs of the Museum Darwinianum.* Moscow, 1935.

Lawlor, M. Cultural influence on preference for design. *Journal of Abnormal and Social Psychology,* Vol. 61, 1955: 680–92.

Morris, D. *The Biology of Art.* New York: Knopf, 1962. P. 135.

Wassef, R. W. *Fleurs du désert.* Paris: Grund, 1961.

——. *Tapisseries de la jeune Égypte.* Paris: Grund, 1972.

CHAPTER FOUR

Céline, L.-F. *Death on the Installment Plan,* trans. by J. H. P. Marks. Boston: Little, Brown, 1938.

Bibliography

Moles, A. *Théorie de l'information et perception esthétique.* Paris: Denoël Gonthier, 1972.

Tomkins, C. Profile: Robert Rauschenberg, *The New Yorker*, February 29, 1964.

CHAPTER FIVE

Charbonnier, G., ed. *Conversations with Claude Lévi-Strauss,* trans. by J. H. and D. Weightman. New York: Grossman, n.d. [1969]. Paperback ed. Pp. 114–15, 122.

Lévi-Strauss, C. *The Savage Mind.* Chicago: University of Chicago Press, 1966.

——. *The Science of Mythology.* Vol. 1: *The Raw and the Cooked.* Vol. 2: *From Honey to Ashes.* New York: Harper & Row, 1970, 1973. Paperback ed.

CHAPTER SIX

Borroff, M. The computer as poet. *Yale Alumni Magazine*, Vol. 34, 1971: 22–25.

Gombrich, E. *Meditations on a Hobby Horse and Other Essays on the Theory of Art.* London: Phaidon, 1971.

Schonberg, H. G. A nice and abstruse game. *Horizon*, Vol. 4, January 1962: 114–20.

CHAPTER SEVEN

Gans, H. *Popular Culture and High Culture.* New York: Basic Books, 1975. Pp. xi, 45.

——, and E. Van Den Haag. Exchange of views, New York *Times*, Arts and Leisure Section, February 9, 1975.

Index

149

Index

Index

aesthetic pleasure and nonsemantic disorder, 104–5
aesthetic response, 99
convention, structure, and form, 99–104, 115
decoration and, 113–14
feeling (subjectively), 106–7
meaning of, 99
modern Western visual art, 106, 108, 116
musical communication, 107–8, 115
religious art, 105
separating art from human-made objects, 109–10
transformation-representations, 110–13, 114–15
Graffiti, 2–3, 19
Graves test, 45

Hamlet (Shakespeare), 73
Happenings, 4, 115–16
Hiroshima, Mon Amour (film), 117, 118
Hirshhorn Museum (Joseph H.), 57, 71
Horizon (magazine), 100
Hyperrealism, 4–5, 91

Icons, 29
Impressionism, 3, 90, 118
"Inauthentic" art, 128
"Infant Ape and Human Child" (Kohts), 52
Information, art and, 57–72
abstract art, 57–58
beauty and "sense," 58–59
communication and language, 59–62
information theory, 63–72
metaphor, 59, 65
public art, 59
semiotic forms, 61–62
visual and auditory communication, 62–64

Ingalik Indians, 10–16, 19, 20
Intermezzo (magazine), 7
Islamic architecture, 114
Iwao, Sumiko, 49

Jazz, 165
Joyce, James, 138

"Kitsch," 128–29
Koch, Kenneth, 53
Kohts, N., 52

Landrover (dance), 9
Langer, Susanne, 40, 62
Lawlor, Monica, 45
Le Monde (newspaper), 6
Lévi-Strauss, Claude, 51, 74 85, 86–88, 89, 90, 91, 92, 93–94, 97, 139
Life and Times of Joseph Stalin, The (Wilson), 10
Literature, structuralism in, 97

Macdonald, Dwight, 129, 136
MacLeish, Archibald, 58
Magician, The (film), 8
Masks, 7, 10–16, 19, 20, 43
Mead, Margaret, 53
Meditations on a Hobby Horse and Other Essays on the Theory of Art (Gombrich), 109
Metaphor, 35, 36, 38–39, 59, 64, 84, 101, 113–14
Minimal art, 4, 116
Moles, Abraham, 66, 68, 70
Moore, Omar Khayyam, 25–27, 28, 54
Morris, Desmond, 31–32, 52–53
Motherwell, Robert, 118
Mozart, Wolfgang Amadeus, 52, 100
Musée de l'Homme (Paris), 30, 150
Music, 107–8, 115, 125, 136
Myth, 33, 43, 116, 139–40
fascination for, 107
structuralism in, 97